AF797902

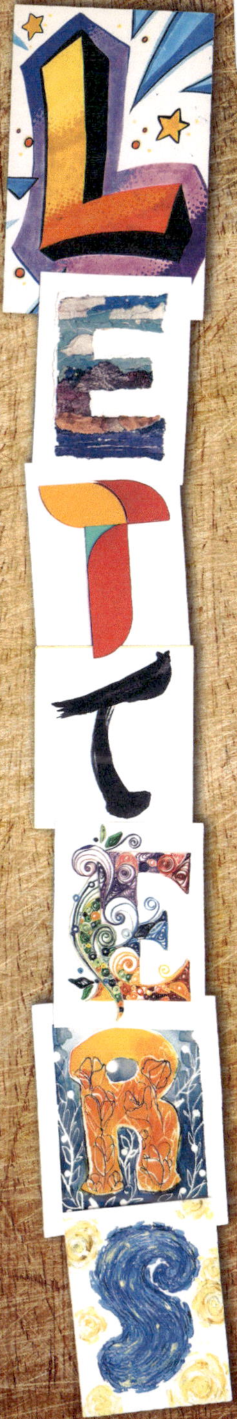

LETTERS

A California Art Anthology

TVWI Book Three

Temecula Valley Writers & Illustrators

TV WI PUBLISHING

LETTERS: A California Art Anthology © 2026 by TVWI

All rights reserved. No part of this book may be reproduced or transmitted in any form or by any means, electronic or mechanical, including photocopying, recording, or by any information storage and retrieval system, nor may the work be used in any manner for purposes of training artificial intelligence technologies to generate images, including, without limitation, technologies that are capable of generating works in the same style(s) as the copyright owners, without the written permission of the publisher.

Cover art & design © 2026 by Amanda Le
Foreword © 2026 by Janice Cipriani-Willis
Supervising Editor Trond E. Hildahl
Layout by Big Giant Media, Inc.

Published by TVWI
30732 Doral Ct
Temecula, CA 92592 (USA)
Published simultaneously worldwide

First Edition
ISBN-13: 979-8-9911302-4-0 (hardcover)
ISBN-13: 979-8-9911302-5-7 (paper)
Library of Congress Control Number: 2026907736

All copyright remains with the original artists, who are the sole copyright owners of the individual works and retain all rights.

"California's Star" © 2026 Alex
"The Hippies of Haight and Ashbury,"
"Snowfall in Mt. Baldy" © 2026 Kimberley Cornell

"Arrowhead Mountain" © 2026 C.Cotter
"Callejón" © 2026 Adam Favela
"Protect Our Ocean Friends" © 2026 Sabin R. Flores
"The Slow Afternoon in Temecula" © 2026 Tiara Harvey
"Blue Skies Ahead," "Neon Sunset,"
"Talent and Trophies" © 2026 Sacha Hope
"California Poppies" © 2026 Amy Huffmire
"The Tree Spirit of Riverside" © 2026 Katinka
"Go-Uh-lden Gate Bridge" © 2026 Alex Kelly
"The Roses in my Garden beneath the Sun" © 2026 Stephenie Bushra Khan
"Grunion Run," "Sailboats on the Bay" © 2026 Amanda Le
"Joshua Tree" © 2026 Kausar P Malik
"EUREKA!" © 2026 Brian Manning
"Saving Sea Life" © 2026 Elizabeth Weimer Marshall
"Hotel Del Coronado, My Hotel California"
"Evening At the Emporium," © 2026 Bonnie Martland
"don't bite the hand that paints you" © 2026 Z Morales
"Garibaldi," "Lizards," "Street Culture,"
"Wine Country" © 2026 Tony Moramarco
"Held Against Time" © 2026 Brooke Olson
"ART/i-fact" © 2026 Kathryn Otoshi
"The unique 'A'rchitecture of California" © 2026 Mary Painter
"Something for Everyone" © 2026 Kai B. Parker
"The Freeways of California,"
"The Trees of California" © 2026 Robert Lewis Rieger
"The Spirit of California Nature" © 2026 Charlie Schimmel
"La Jolla Leopard Sharks" © 2026 Stefanie Schonleber
"Lizards of California" © 2026 Madeline Secules
"S," "Tidepools" © 2026 Michael Smith
"Central California Coast," "Elephant Seals" © 2026 John Waddleton
"Hollywood Ratings" © 2026 Erin Warren
"Eureka" © 2026 Robin Wesley

Dedication

What you're holding in your hands isn't just a collection of individual pieces. It reflects what can happen when diverse artists come together to answer a call—exchanging ideas, testing concepts, and allowing their work to grow toward something greater than the sum of its parts.

At TVWI, we see this phenomenon play out again and again within our talented corps of creatives. We've found that when a space like ours exists, the work stops feeling guardrailed or constrained. Instead, it starts to breathe, adding greater depth and scope. And before long, it's grown past what any one person could've made alone. That's the beauty of creative community.

So, we offer this to all creatives—if you've spent years working quietly alone, or if you're just beginning to find your footing—if you've ever faced a blank canvas, a clean page, or an empty, glowing screen completely on your own, you know the feeling. The urge to create something is powerful, but it's also difficult. The good news is, it never has to be undertaken alone. We know that art will always be most rewarding when shared, with allies, advocates, associates, and friends. This is our proof.

Consider this our letter to you.

Table of Contents

Foreword xiii

Introduction 1

Something for Everyone
(Kai B. Parker) 6

The unique "A"rchitecture of California
(Mary Painter) 8

The Tree Spirit of Riverside
(Katinka) 10

Evening at the Emporium
(Bonnie Martland) 12

The Trees of California
(Robert Lewis Rieger) 14

Saving Sea Life
(Elizabeth Weimer Marshall) 16

Central California Coast
(John Waddleton) 18

Roses
(Stephenie Bushra Khan) 20

California Poppies
(Amy Huffmire) 22

Street Culture
(Tony Moramarco) 24

Talent and Trophies
(Sacha Hope) 26

EUREKA!
(Brian Manning) 28

ART/i-fact
(Kathryn Otoshi) 30

Hollywood Ratings
(Erin Warren) 32

Tidepools
(Michael Smith) 34

Neon Sunset
(Sacha Hope) 36

Sailboats on the Bay
(Amanda Le) 38

The Slow Afternoon in Temecula
(Tiara Harvey) 40

The Hippies of Haight and Ashbury
(Kimberley Cornell) 42

Lizards of California
(Madeline Secules) 44

La Jolla Leopard Sharks
(Stefanie Schonleber) 46

Arrowhead Mountain
(C. Cotter) 48

The Spirit of California Nature
(Charlie Schimmel) 50

Grunion Run
(Amanda Le) 52

Go-Uh-lden Gate Bridge
(Alex Kelly) 54

don't bite the hand that paints you
(Z Morales) 56

Garibaldi
(Tony Moramarco) 58

Eureka
(Robin Wesley) 60

Protect Our Ocean Friends
(Sabin R. Flores) 62

The Freeways of California
(Robert Lewis Rieger) 64

Joshua Tree
(Kausar P Malik)........66

Hotel Del Coronado, My Hotel California
(Bonnie Martland)........68

Wine Country
(Tony Moramarco)........70

Snowfall in Mt. Baldy
(Kimberley Cornell)........72

Blue Skies Ahead
(Sacha Hope)........74

Callejón
(Adam Favela)........76

Held Against Time
(Brooke Olson)........78

Lizards
(Tony Moramarco)........80

Elephant Seals
(John Waddleton)........82

"S"
(Michael Smith)........84

California's Star
(Alex)........86

About the Artists........88

Acknowledgments........98

Thank you... 99

Foreword

Welcome to LETTERS, a project that celebrates the spirit of California.

The invited curator for this anthology, I took great joy in watching the artists of Temecula Valley Writers and Illustrators capture the essence of my home state. I believe art has a purpose beyond its own beauty: bringing people together and bridging our different lives and stories. Paint, ink, and now digital art delight our senses and help us see the world through someone else's eyes.

In these pages, you'll find the magnificent trees, the restless coast, the varied fauna, and the striking architecture that make California so unique. This collection shows that art is a vital part of what makes our communities unique and this state feel like our home. I am so proud of the book this group has crafted, and I hope these illustrations move you as much as they have inspired me. I invite you to turn the page and be dazzled at the beauty of our Golden State.

Janice Cipriani-Willis

Temecula, California

April, 2026

Introduction

Art is inherent to everything we do as a species.

Give a child a crayon and you know what's going to happen to your walls. Grab a pencil while you're bored on that conference call and you'll hang up thirty doodles later. And when you finally let yourself take a class, or check out that "How to Draw" book from the library? That's the good stuff. Soul-satisfying stuff.

Here in Temecula Valley Writers and Illustrators, our own artists clamored for more after illustrating the short stories in Volumes 1 & 2. In fact, they made a convincing argument for their own book!

We challenged our illustrators in two ways. First, to reveal what they adore about our home state of California. And second, to spell out the phrase DARE TO CREATE: ART IS THE LANGUAGE OF THE FEARLESS, one letter at a time.

And so, LETTERS was born. We hope you enjoy this gorgeous paean to the Golden State and artistic expression.

By the way? Those are magnificent doodles. Dare to take another class. Dare to practice.

Dare to create.

The Board of Directors

Temecula Valley Writers and Illustrators

Creativity in Community

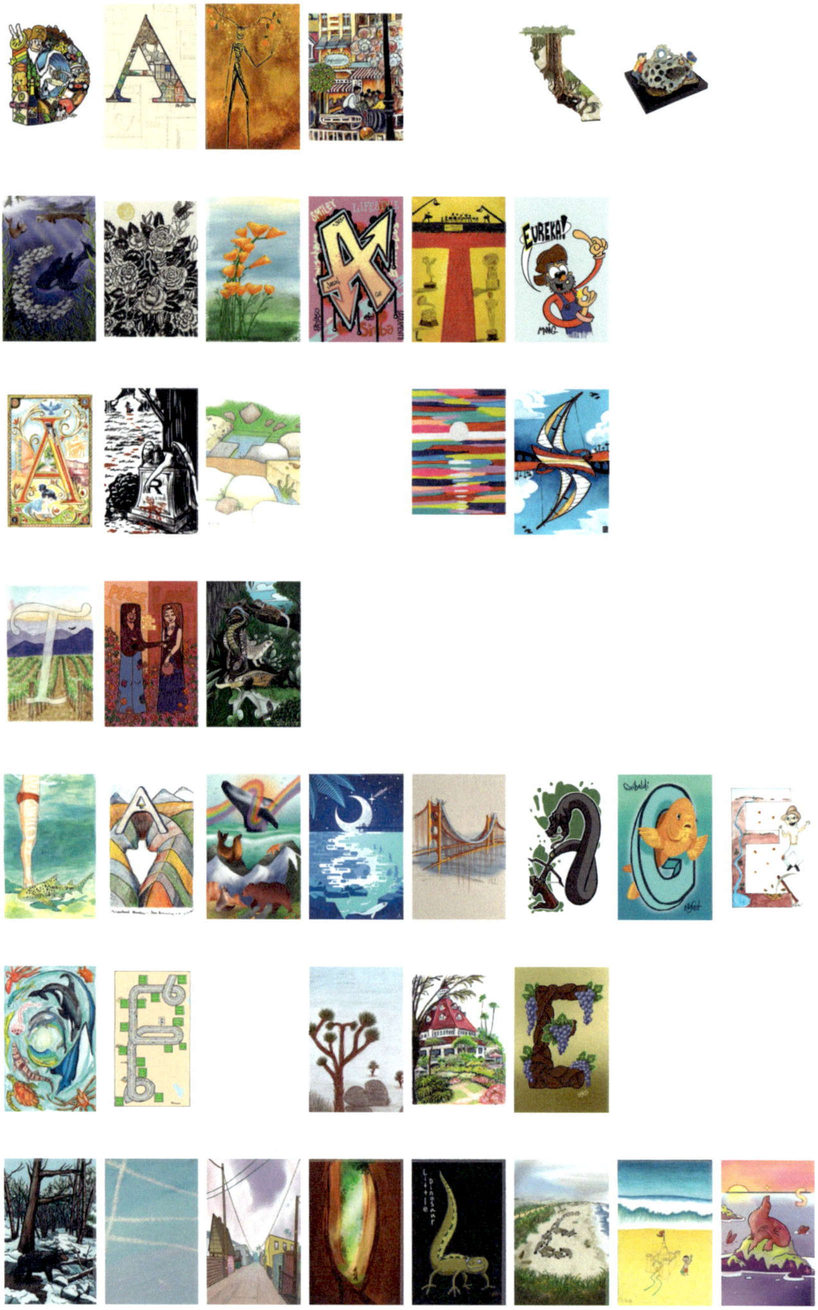
EUREKA!

DARE TO
CREATE
ART IS
THE
LANGUAGE
OF THE
FEARLESS

And now, how the artists responded...

The goal with this piece was to highlight all that California has to offer. It's the only place you can do things like see a Lakers Game, go snowboarding, surf, and attend a movie premiere on the same day without driving more than a couple of hours. I also used the illustration to mirror locations geographically, with SoCal along the bottom, moving up through Central California and into NorCal.

Something for Everyone

Digital

Letter: D

Kai B. Parker

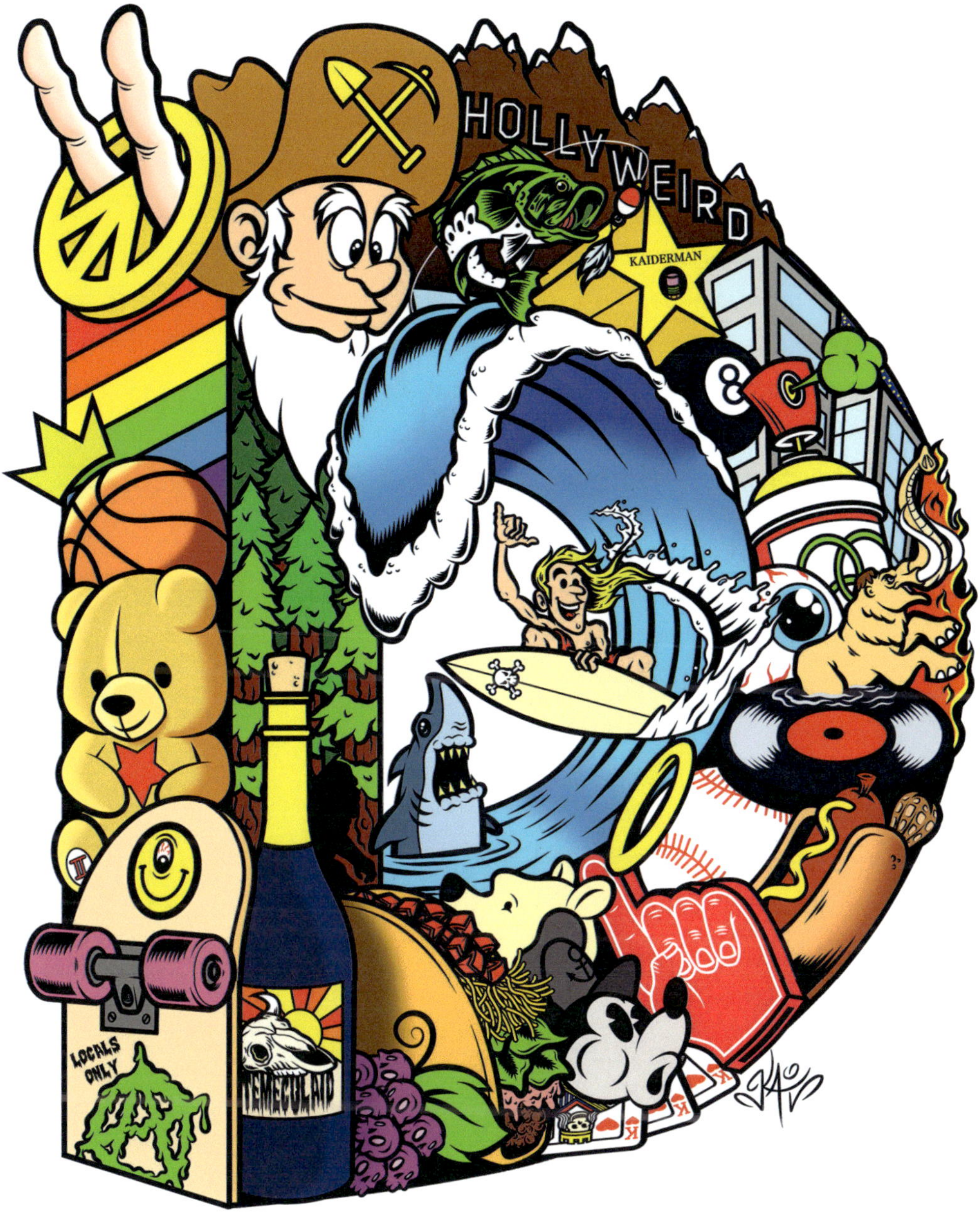
HOLLYWEIRD
KAIDERMAN
LOCALS ONLY
TEMECULAID

As a lover of art and architecture, I wanted to highlight California State's iconic buildings and landmarks up and down the coast. The architects behind each building were fearless for their time when creating their designs, whether through material or form. This piece aims to not only celebrate the wide range of architectural styles in California but also to spark a fearless adventure for the viewer to experience these structures in person (or find their favorite in the illustration).

SOME BUILDING HINTS: STAHL HOUSE, DISNEY MUSIC CONCERT HALL
BACKGROUND: A HAND-DRAWN AMALGAMATION OF DIFFERENT FLOOR PLANS BASED ON ALL FEATURED BUILDINGS.

The unique "A"rchitecture of California
Traditional pen and ink on MD paper
Letter: A
Mary Painter

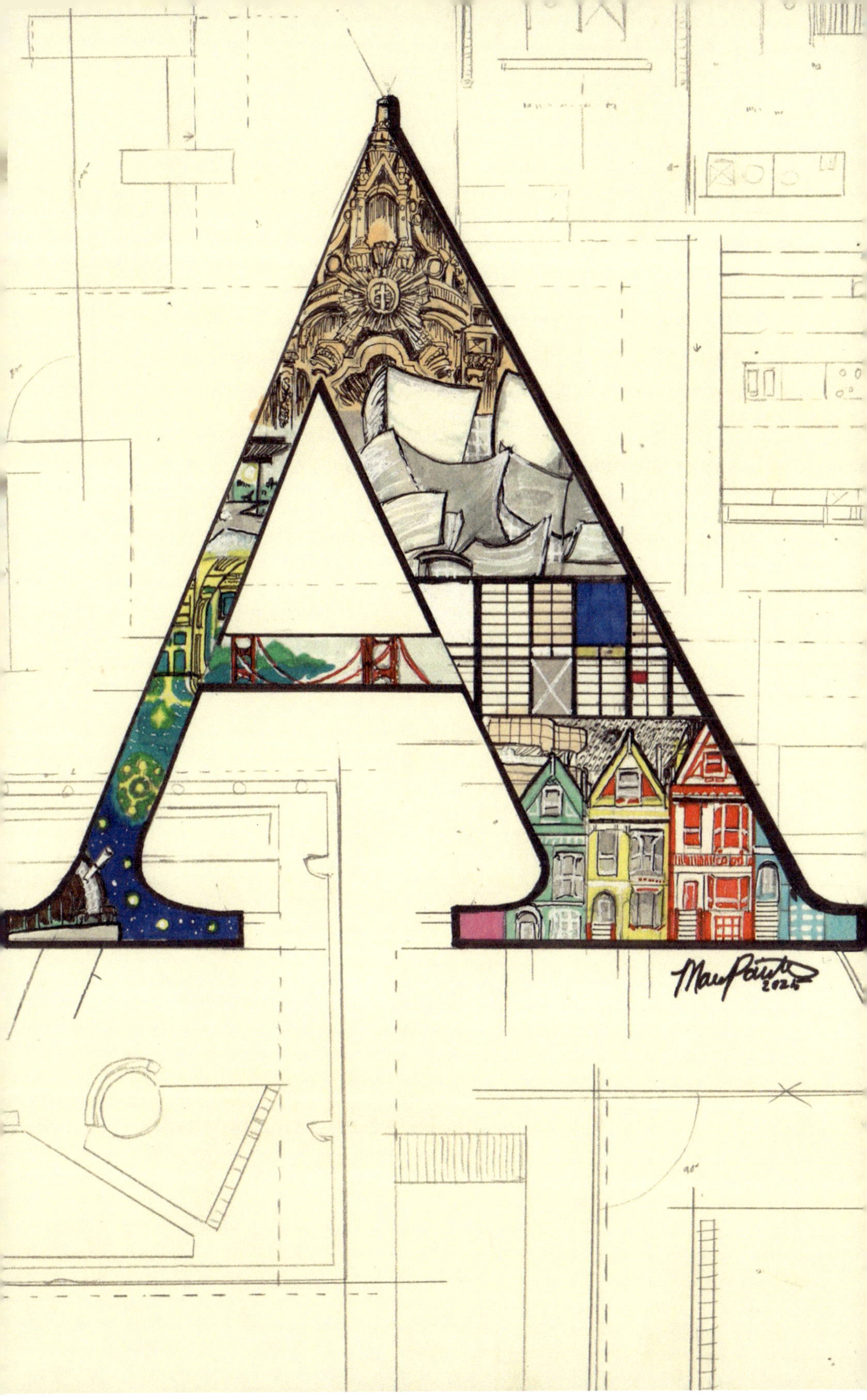

This one is an orange tree spirit and represents the history of citrus in California. Two navel orange trees arrived from Brazil to Riverside in the 1870s. All the navel orange trees in California are descended from those same two trees. One of the trees is still alive in Riverside 150 years later. Riverside is also home to the Noah's Ark of Citrus at UC Riverside, hosting two of each of the more than 2600 varieties of citrus in the world.

The Tree Spirit of Riverside

Acrylic

Letter: R

Katinka

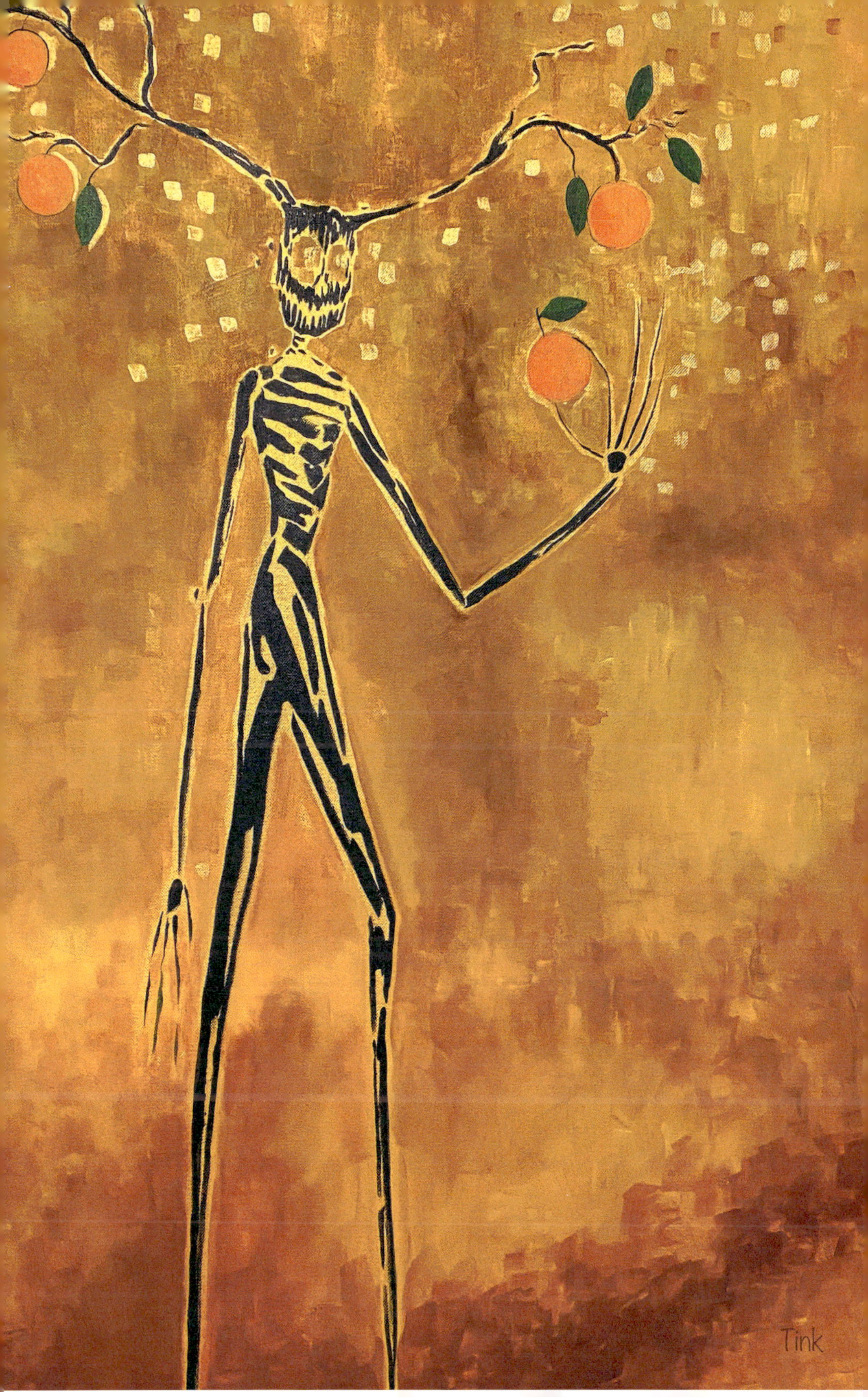
Tink

Disneyland has always inspired me. We visited the year it opened. I worked there while in high school and college. One of my first jobs was at the Emporium on Main Street. Walt Disney would visit during Christmas. While there, I was encouraged with a big box of cells sent from the Disney Studios and a letter urging me to continue creating. The Emporium block still generates a sense of nostalgia for America's past while lifting my spirits with the urge and energy to "dare to create" something new. When thinking of iconic California, I had to include the Emporium.

Evening at the Emporium

Quick sketch in acrylic gouache, colored pencil and ink.

Letter: E

Bonnie Martland

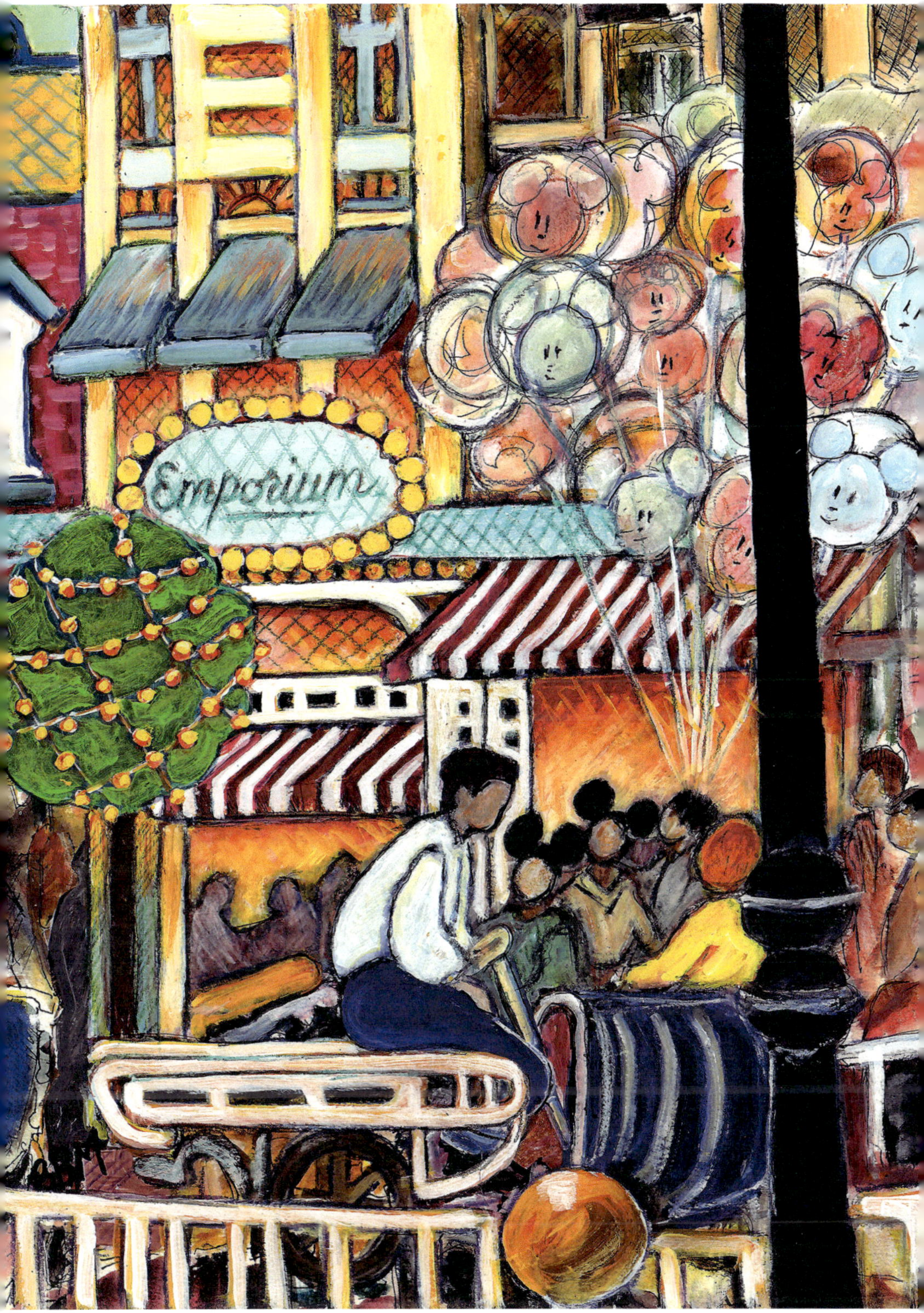
Emporium

I recently visited Sequoia National Park, Yosemite National Park and other areas of California. The breathtaking views of the impressive giant sequoias, the extensive forests of evergreens and the sheer number of different varieties of trees throughout the state made an indelible impression on me. No words of mine can sufficiently describe what my eyes could see, and no work of art can adequately portray their beauty and stature. But as I bore witness to this national treasure, I hope my tribute to them raises awareness that our California forests and groves of trees must always be protected.

The Trees of California

Digital Art

Letter: T

Robert Lewis Rieger

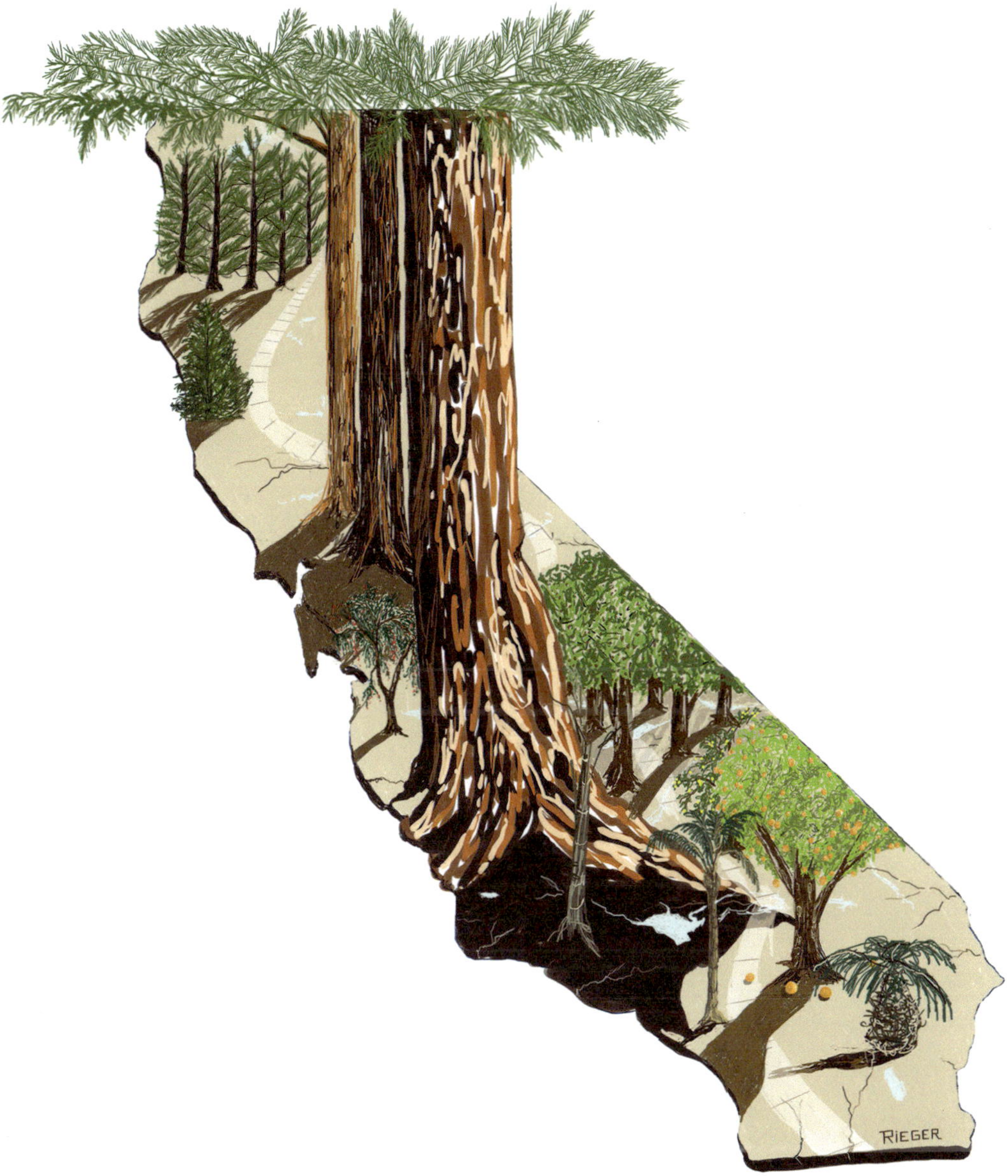
RIEGER

There are three major organizations in California dedicated to saving sea turtles, yet it is still never enough. Only 1 in 1,000 hatchlings survive to adulthood—a staggering reality noted by Greater Good Charities. Creating my piece "Saving Sea Life" was my way of reminding the public how urgently our beaches and wildlife need protection.

This work calls on all of us to care for our California coastline: to avoid leaving trash behind, to volunteer when we can, and to protect the fragile sea life that depends on us.

Saving Sea Life
Ceramic / wood base
Letter: O
Elizabeth Weimer Marshall

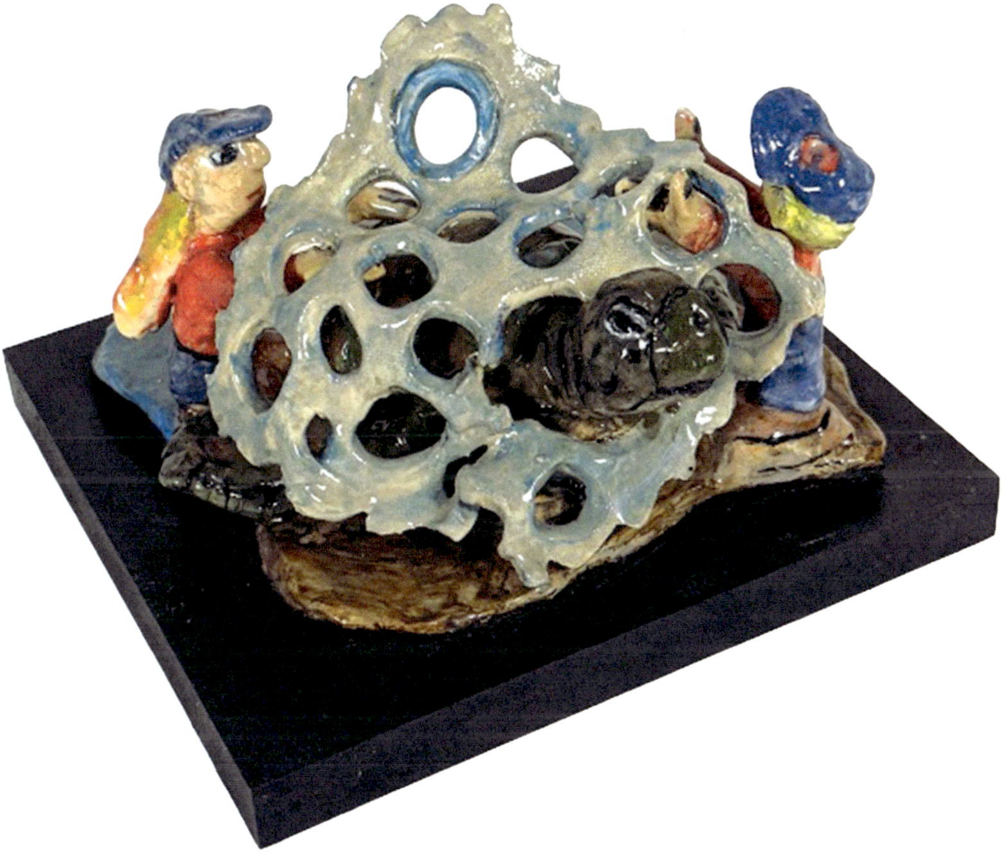

Under the Bay in Monterey!

A bevy of marine mammals frolic in the waters off the coast of central California.

Central California Coast
Digital Drawing on Sketchbook Pro for iPad
Letter: C
John Waddleton

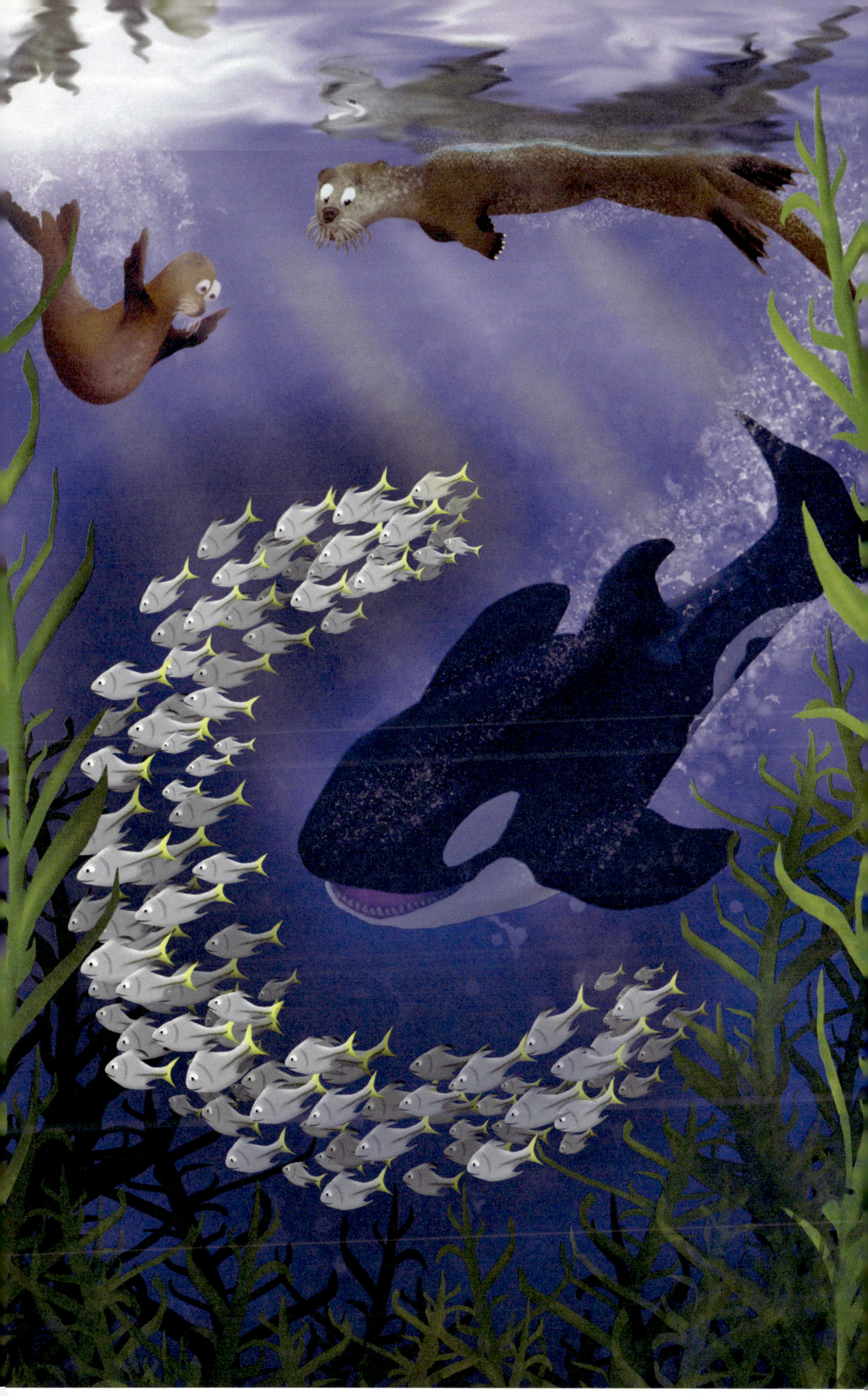

California is the perfect place to grow roses almost year-round, either underground irrigation or watered every day. Hybrid roses grow easily here, and with care, can grow thick and tall with big blooms. I totally enjoy taking care of my roses in my backyard. I have a variety of different colored roses that have different scents. There is something very spiritual for me taking care of my roses.

Throughout the centuries they have been used in many spiritual settings and have spiritual and romantic symbolism. Their scents and perfume have been used in religious rituals. Also, they are the flowers given to friends and lovers. The blooms can be eaten and cooked with—I have made rose jelly and rose scones. In April, here in Southern California, they bloom abundantly and are beautiful to admire and look at. I love to sit outside to observe them and enjoy their visual beauty and scent.

Roses
Pen and ink
Letter: R
Stephenie Bushra Khan

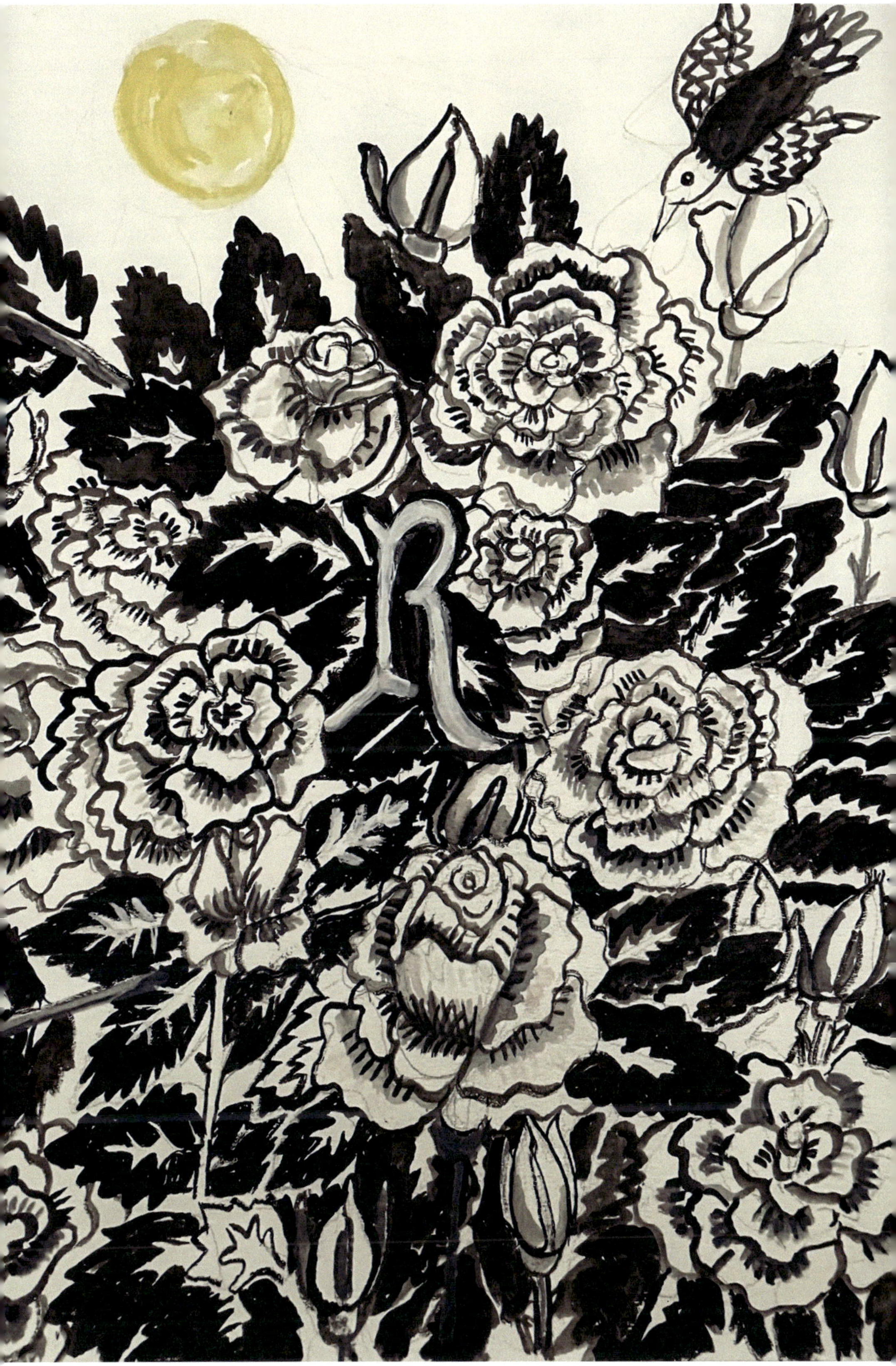
R

I chose California poppies for their quiet beauty. They can surprise you with a splash of color where you least expect it, making you pause to admire nature's artwork. At the right time, an empty field transforms into a sea of gold when the blooms emerge. Up close, each flower is a delicate treasure.

California Poppies
Digital
Letter: E
Amy Huffmire

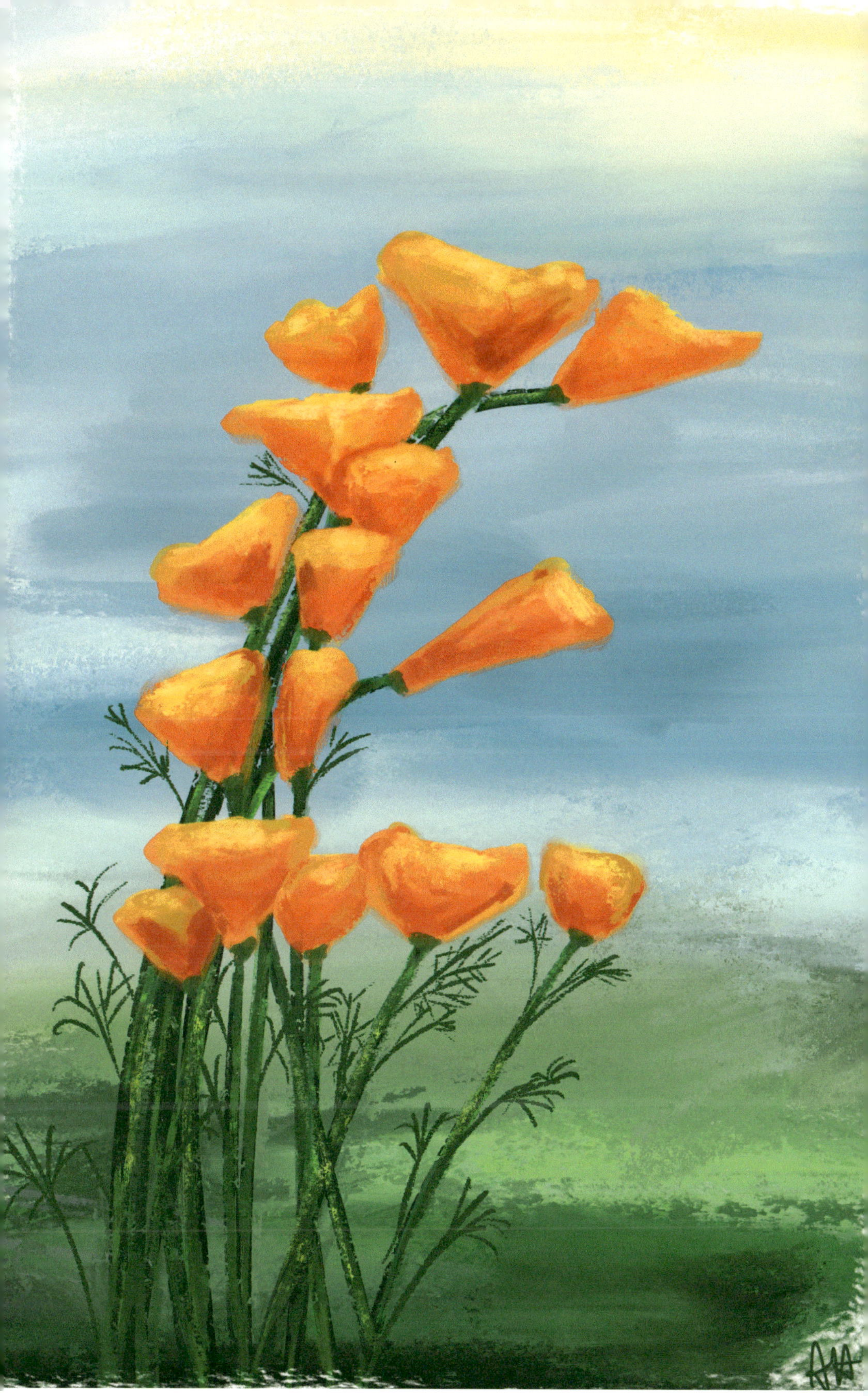

From inner cities to rural towns all throughout California, artists are literally taking their creativity to the streets. Street Art has a unique history. If you pay attention, you can see the progression from beginner taggers to more experienced masters of their craft.

The best of this discipline are now selling their Art & Designs for millions of dollars. This piece is an homage to this unique and colorful art form.

Street Culture
Digital Art / ProCreate
Letter: A
Tony Moramarco

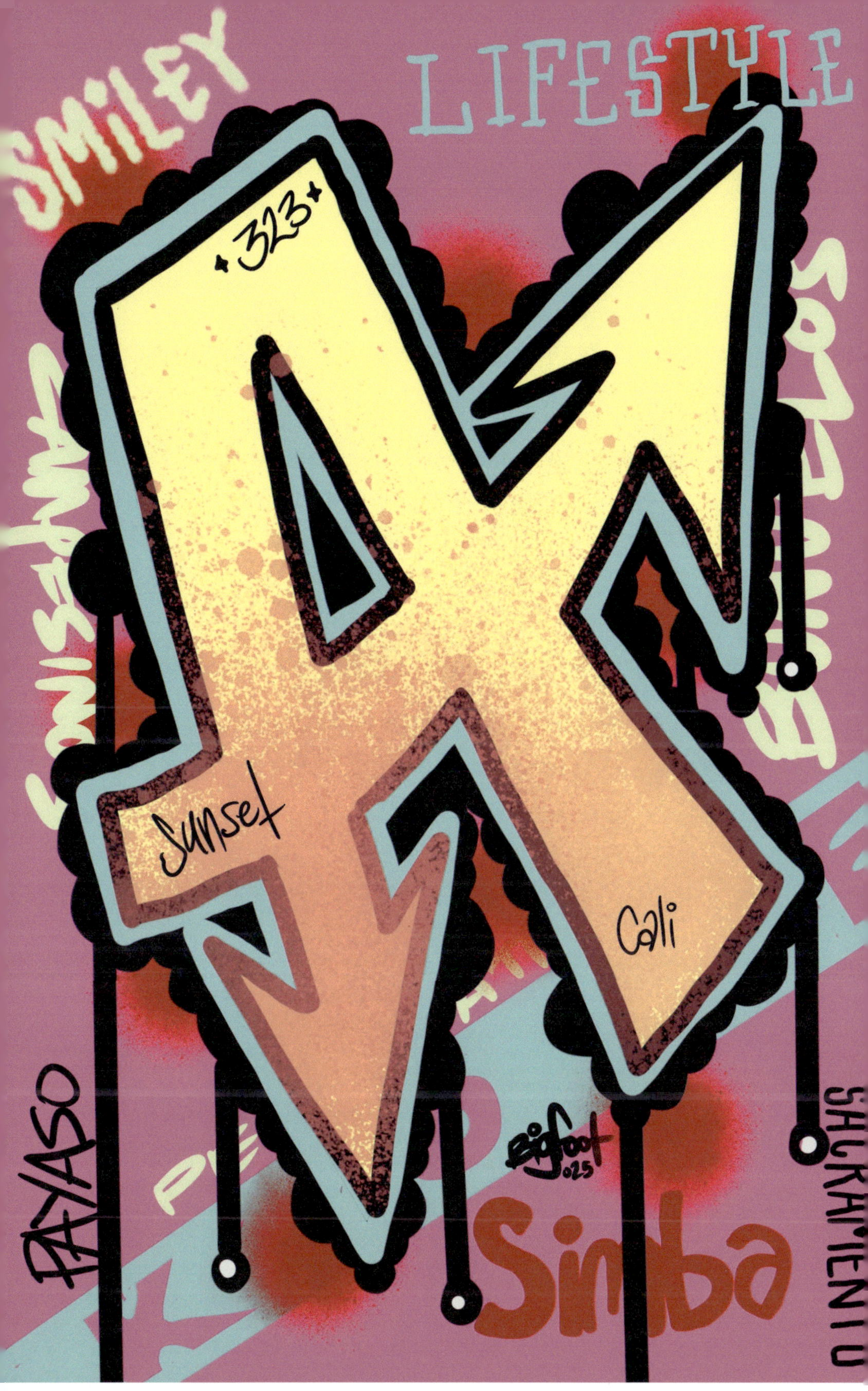
SMILEY
LIFESTYLE
323
Sunset
Cali
Bigfoot
025
PAYASO
SACRAMENTO
Simba

California is a melting pot full of creatives. Musicians, actors, directors, writers, stylists and artists all filter through at some time or another.

We celebrate, and we sure love to give out trophies. Not everyone gets to walk a red carpet, but I'll tell you what, if you ever do—it's pretty epic!

Talent and Trophies
Acrylic on canvas
Letter: T
Sacha Hope

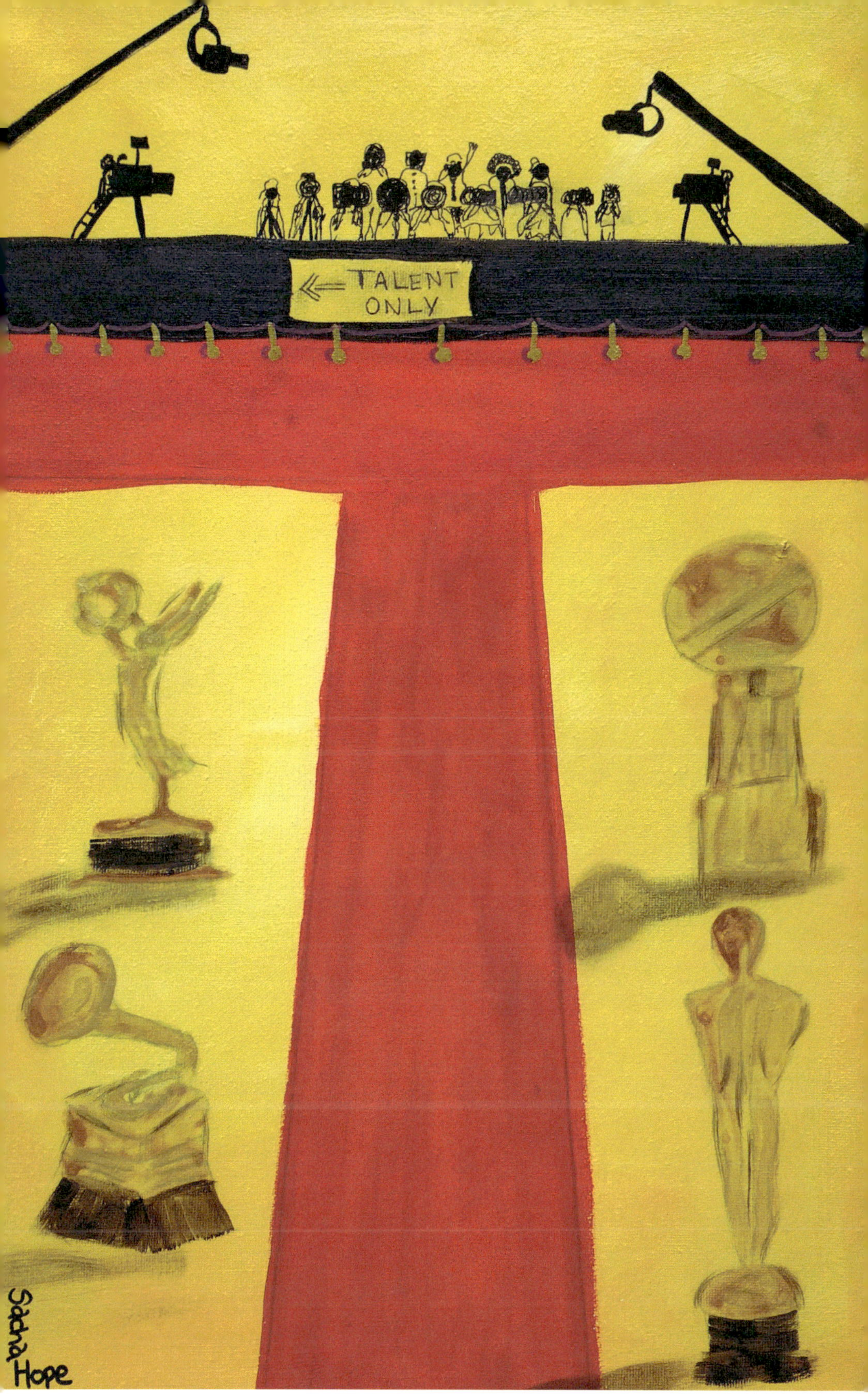

TALENT
ONLY
Sacha-Hope

An old prospector finds gold and screams, “EUREKA!!”—Greek for “I found it!” and the State Motto.

EUREKA!
Hand drawn and colored through Procreate
Letter: E
Brian Manning

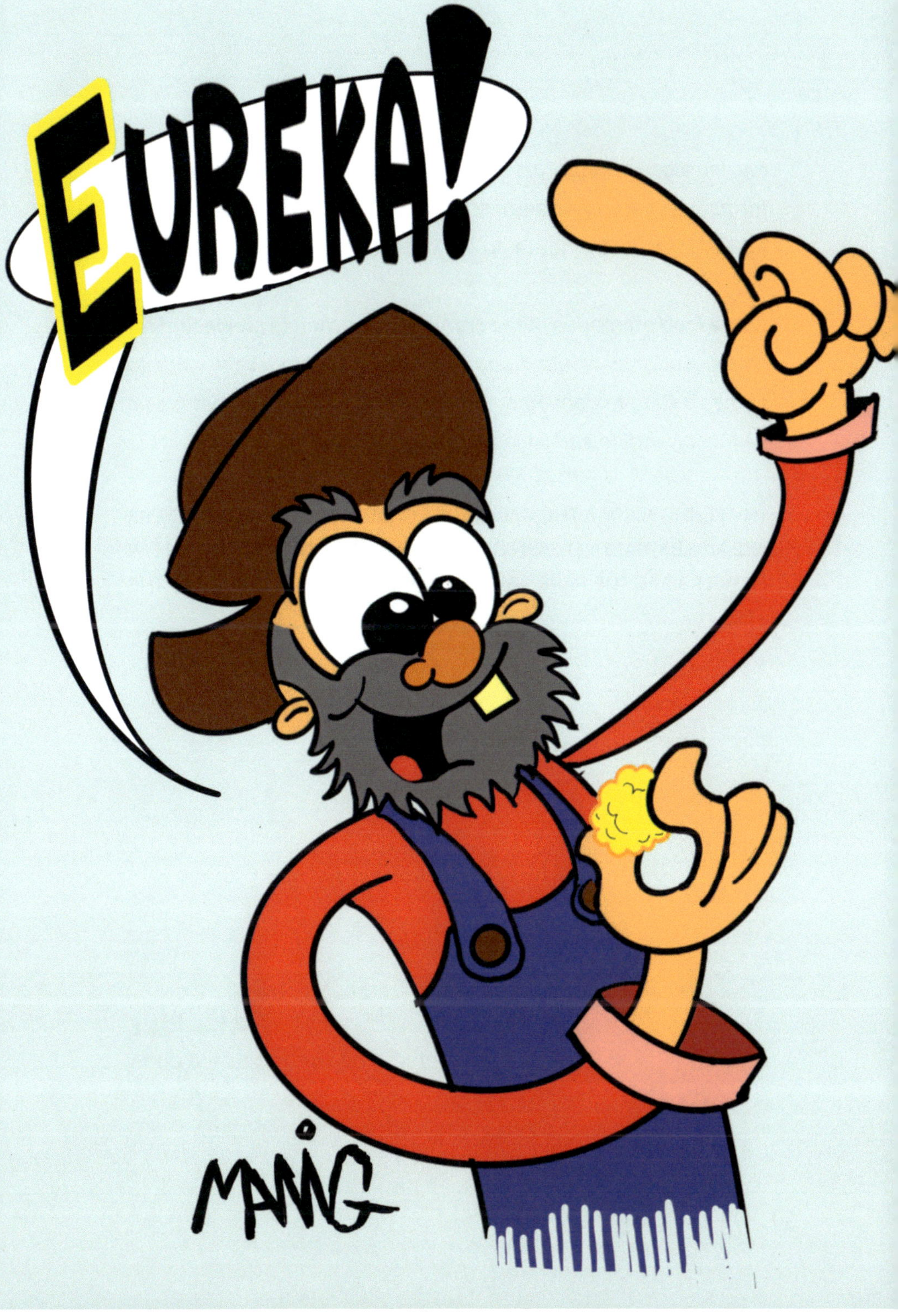
EUREKA!
MANIG

My decision to pursue art is a choice I will always be proud of. My formative years as a design student at Cal Poly, San Luis Obispo ('85-91) was instrumental to my growth as an artist.

I have fond memories of the Fremont, an arthouse movie theater many students would frequent. After the film, we'd walk to Linnea's Cafe to converse and sketch. Off campus, there was a variety of wildlife and vegetation to draw inspiration from.

THE FLYING BIRD IS THE CALIFORNIA SCRUB JAY. THE RED FLOWERS ARE MY ABSTRACT VERSION OF THE RED MARIPOSA LILY. THE YELLOW FLOWERS ARE THE RARE SAN LUIS MARIPOSA LILY, ENDEMIC TO THE AREA.

ART/i-fact
Watercolors and water-soluble pens
Letter: A
Kathryn Otoshi

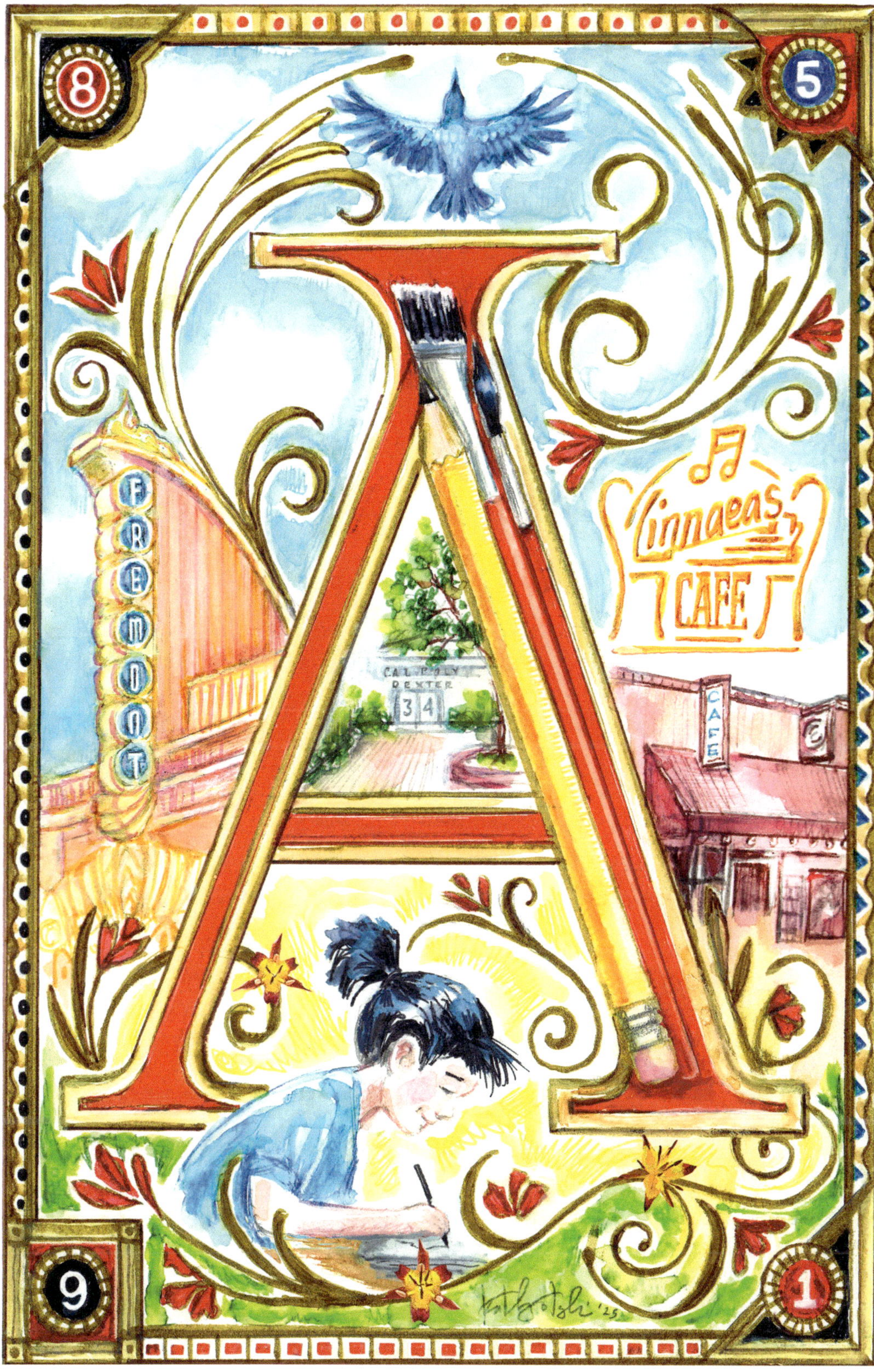

8
5
9
1
FREMONT
Linnaeas
CAFE
CAL POLY
DEXTER
34
CAFE

I themed the art after California's famous Hollywood movies, which often contain mystery, intrigue, and tragedy. Big movies are often rated R for their graphic imagery.

Hollywood Ratings
Digital
Letter: R
Erin Warren

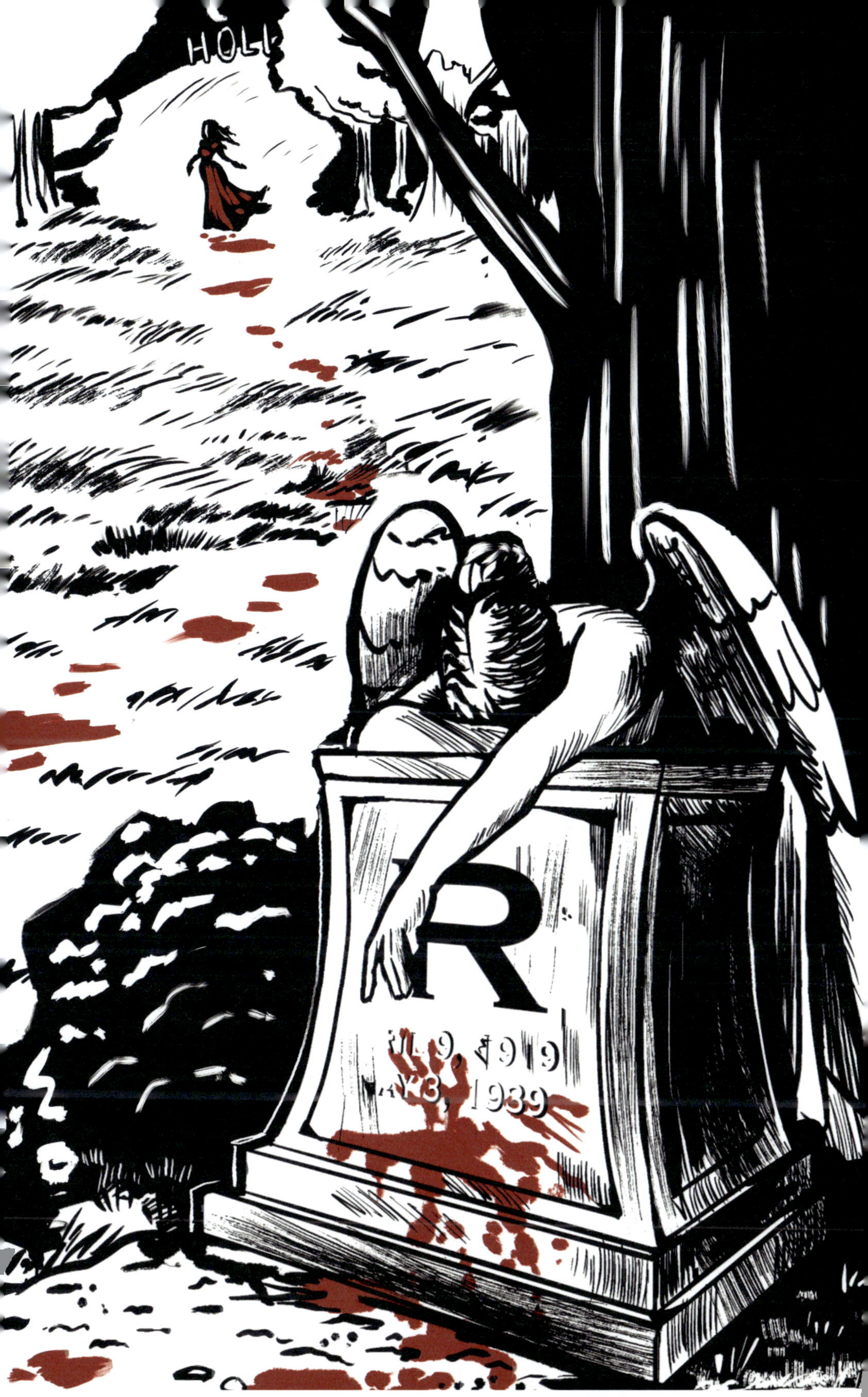
HOLL
R
3, 1939

“My bare feet stopped walking once the rocks became slippery. High tide refilled its pools then withdrew. Down on one knee, looking at the miniature water world below, a slow-motion drama played out in the saltwater shallows.

Taking another knee and more time to watch an octopus arm unfold, extend, searching. A crab walks perpendicularly in the wrong direction. The back of my neck turns a bright red and I’m oblivious.

Tidepools
Colored pencil/ink
Letter: T
Michael Smith

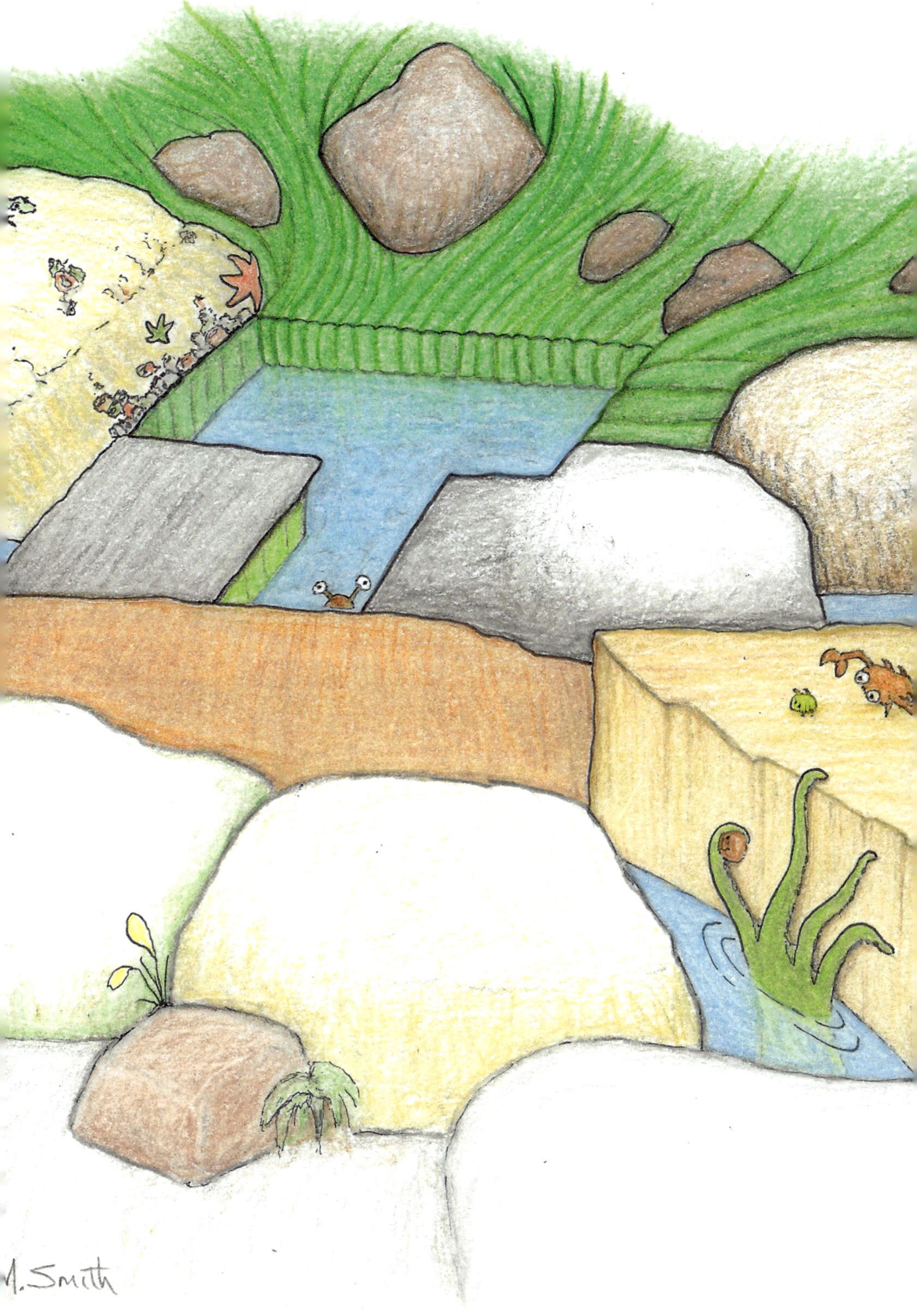
M. Smith

Sunsets along the coast are full of luminous color, dramatic lines, and hypnotic vibes.

I never miss a chance to watch a sunset. It is a kiss goodbye from another beautiful day in paradise.

Neon Sunset
Acrylic on 11x14 Cotton Canvas
Letter: I
Sacha Hope

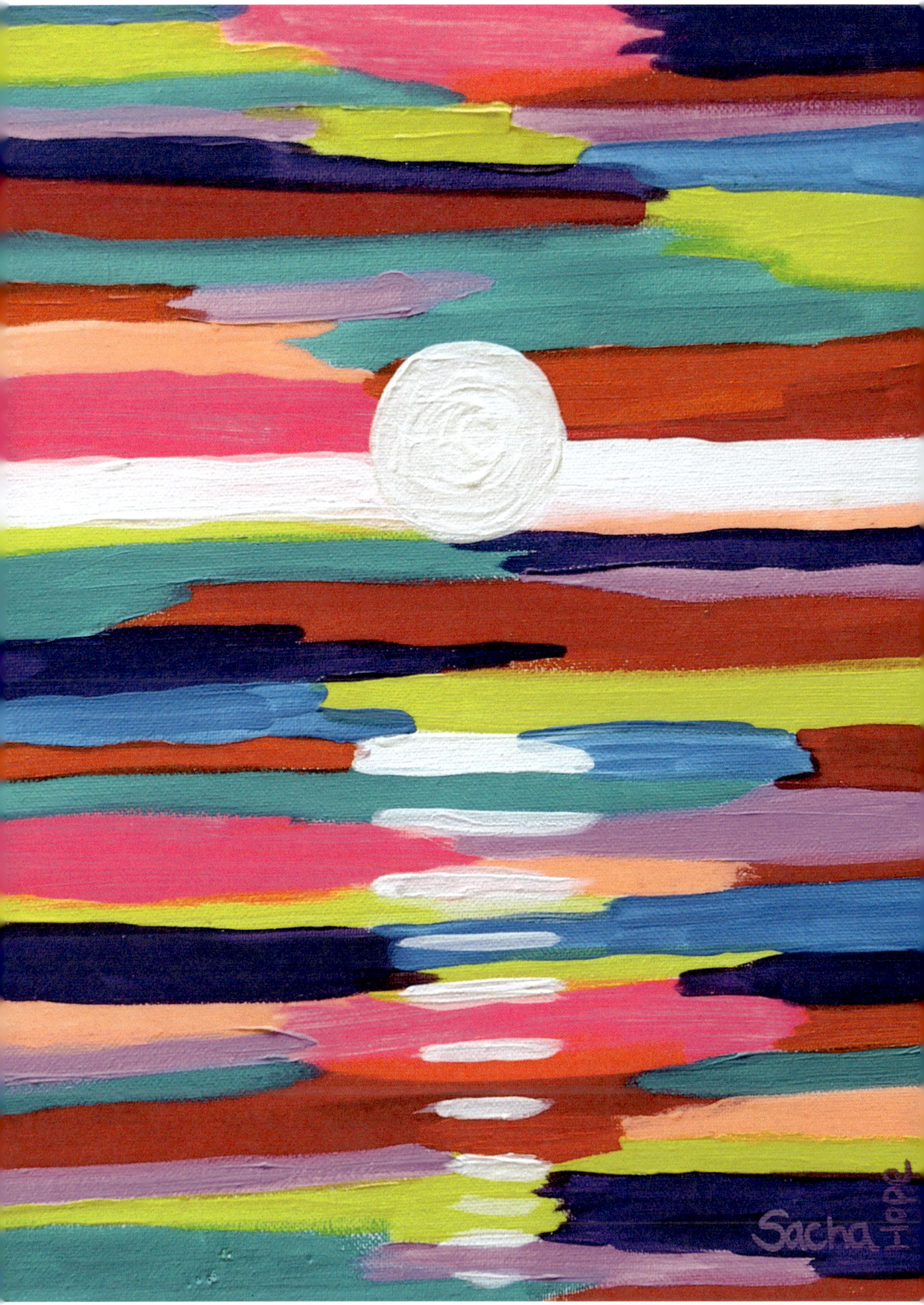
Sacha Hope

My high school was just a walk away from the San Diego Bay. My friends and I would go out to watch the sailboats, take our shoes off, and frolic on the rocky shores. I painted my first plein airs there and learned to look up at the world. The bridge was visible from my corner of the bay, along with the iconic coastal palm trees and seagulls.

I used oranges and yellows to reflect the warmth and nostalgia I feel when I return to the bay, and as a complement to the brilliant blue of the sea and sky.

Sailboats on the Bay
Goache, Watercolor, India Ink
Letter: S
Amanda Le

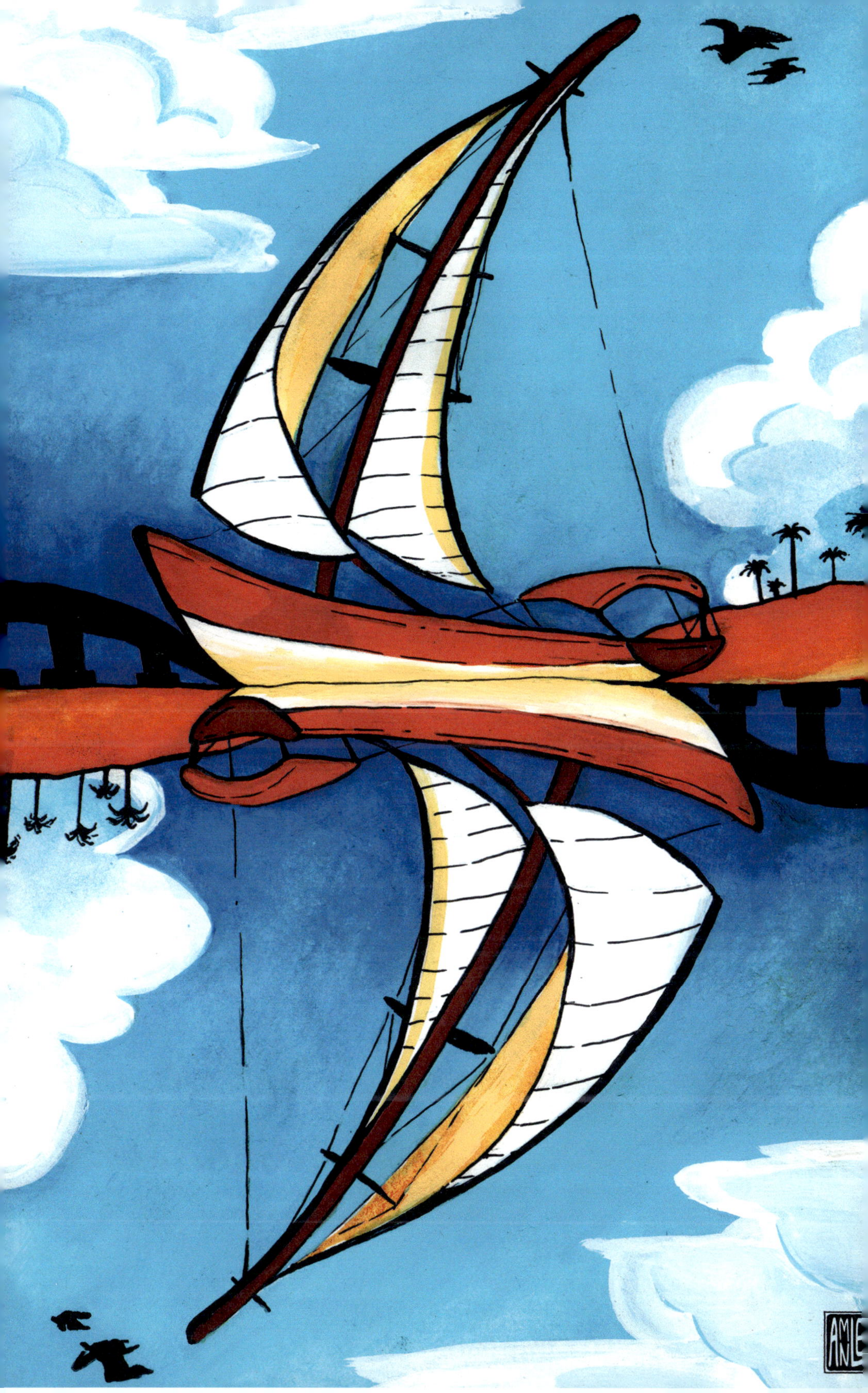

I am always in awe of the scenery in our area and chose to focus on a few of the beautiful things I get to enjoy every day that represent the Temecula Valley.

The Slow Afternoon in Temecula

Watercolor

Letter: T

Tiara Harvey

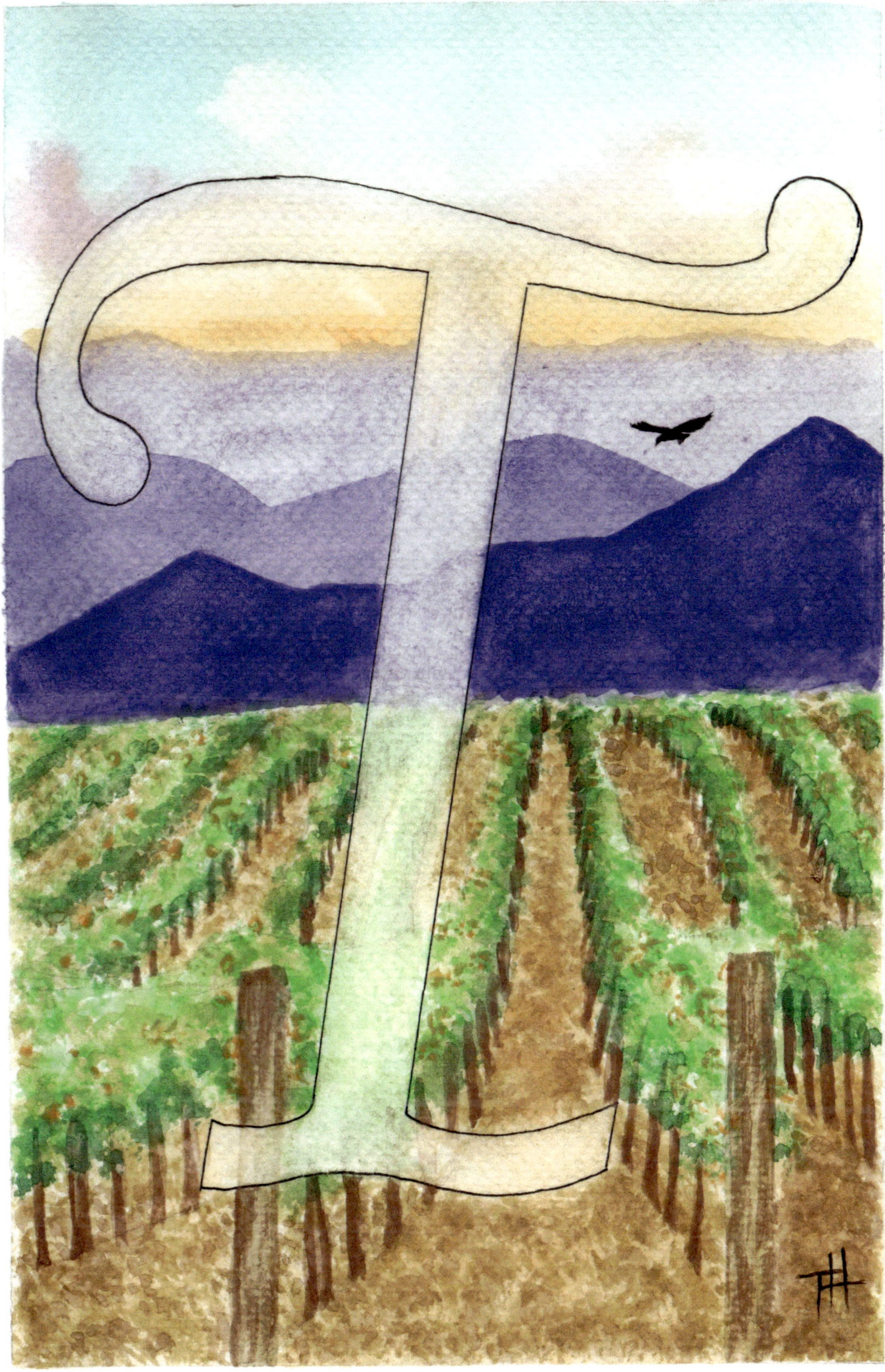

“The Hippies of Haight and Ashbury” was inspired by the historical and cultural influence of hippies in California. For the artwork itself, I drew inspiration from the aspects of hippie culture that I appreciate, such as the music, fashion, enjoyment of nature, and art. The style of the illustration is based on the colorful psychedelic band and concert posters of the 1960s. The color palette contains warmer tones to represent the warmth and good vibes often associated with hippies. The setting of the artwork is the famous street corner where Haight and Ashbury intersect. The flower children (also known as hippies) loved flowers and used them frequently as symbols and motifs. The flowers included in the scene showcase native California plants while representing their significance to the counterculture. Each of these elements were used to create an art piece that embodies the carefree and easy-going nature of hippie culture that harkens to the freedom of one’s spirit and the creativity of self-expression.

The Hippies of Haight and Ashbury

Digital

Letter: H

Kimberley Cornell

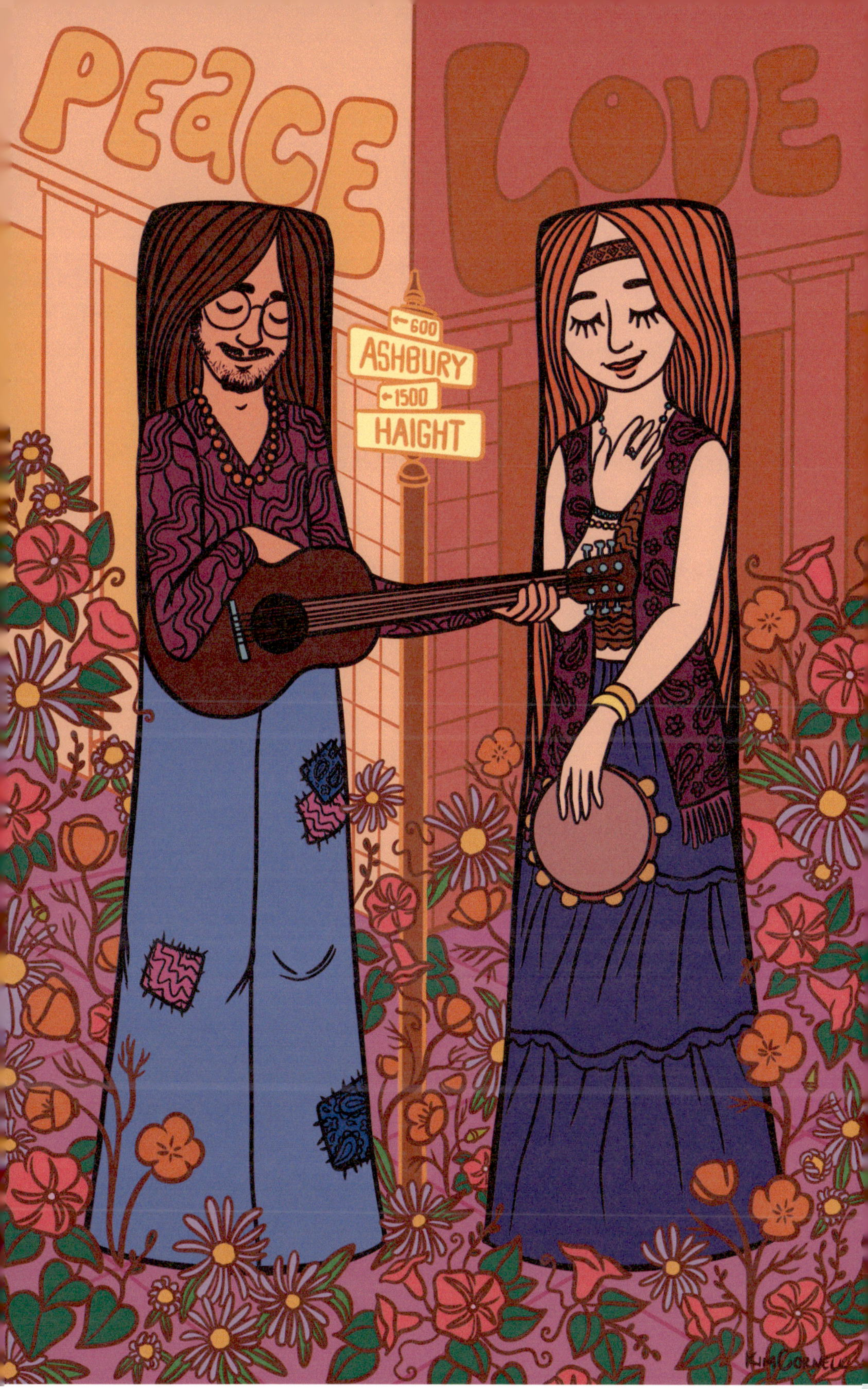
PEACE
LOVE
600
ASHBURY
1500
HAIGHT
KIM CORNELL

This piece was inspired by the many memories I have of chasing and catching lizards with my younger siblings.

No matter where we were, backyard, park, grandparent's house: where there were rocks there were lizards, and where there were lizards, there we were as well.

And while I haven't encountered every lizard I've depicted here, nor is this an exhaustive list, there are a few that remind me very strongly of growing up in SoCal, that I have taken the time to illustrate.

Like the Southern Alligator Lizard, and the Western Fence Lizard.

I'll never forget getting bit.

Lizards of California
Digital Illustration (ClipStudioPaint)
Letter: E
Madeline Secules

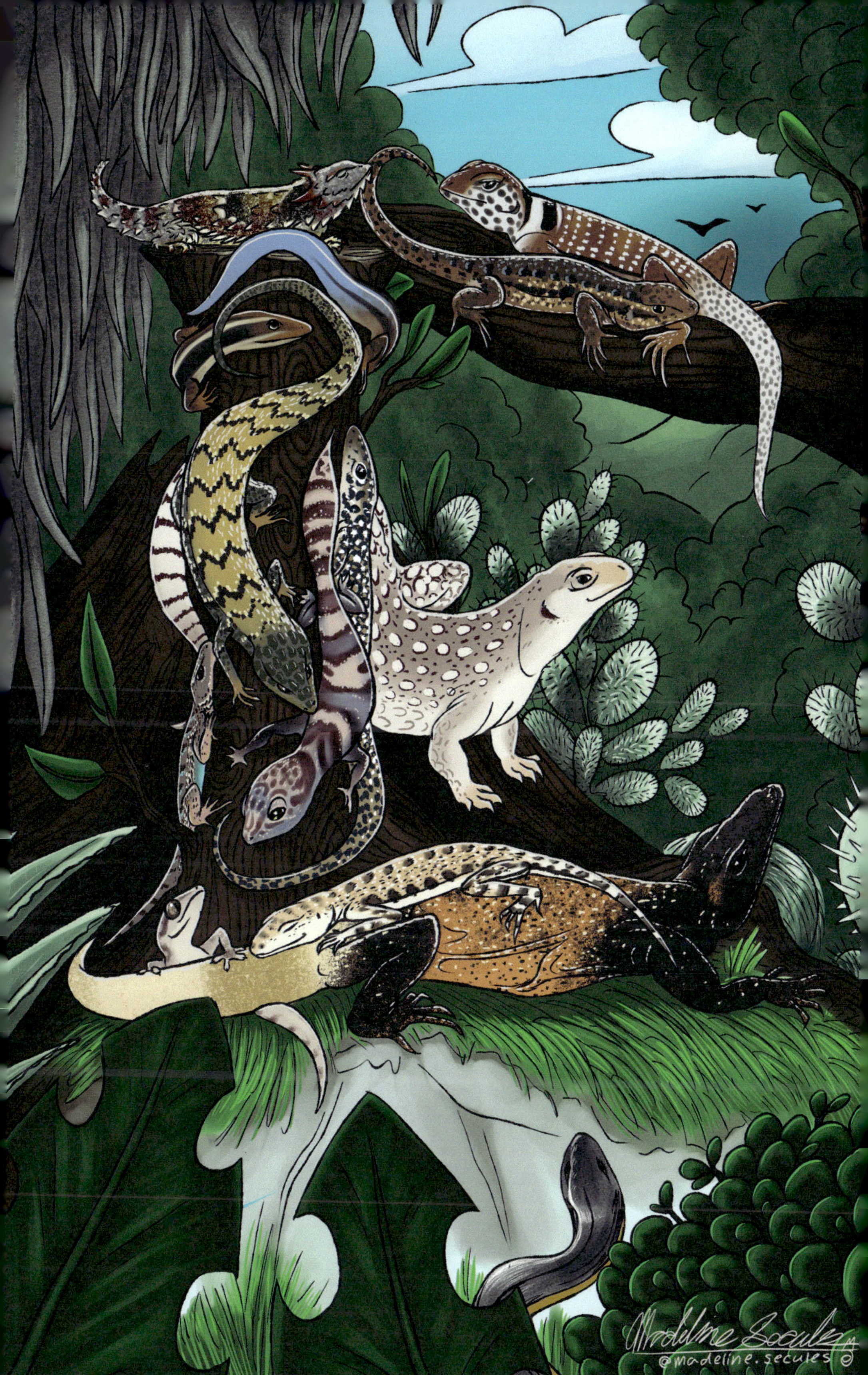
@madeline.secules

The familiar beauty of the California coastline, especially La Jolla, holds a secret: a peaceful, seasonal convergence. Countering the primal fear sharks often instill, this work celebrates the annual gathering of a highly docile species that swims in close proximity to humans while nursing its embryos. The work stands as a testament to the falsehood of our conditioned fears, celebrating an extraordinary peaceful equilibrium.

La Jolla Leopard Sharks

Watercolor

Letter: L

Stefanie Schonleber

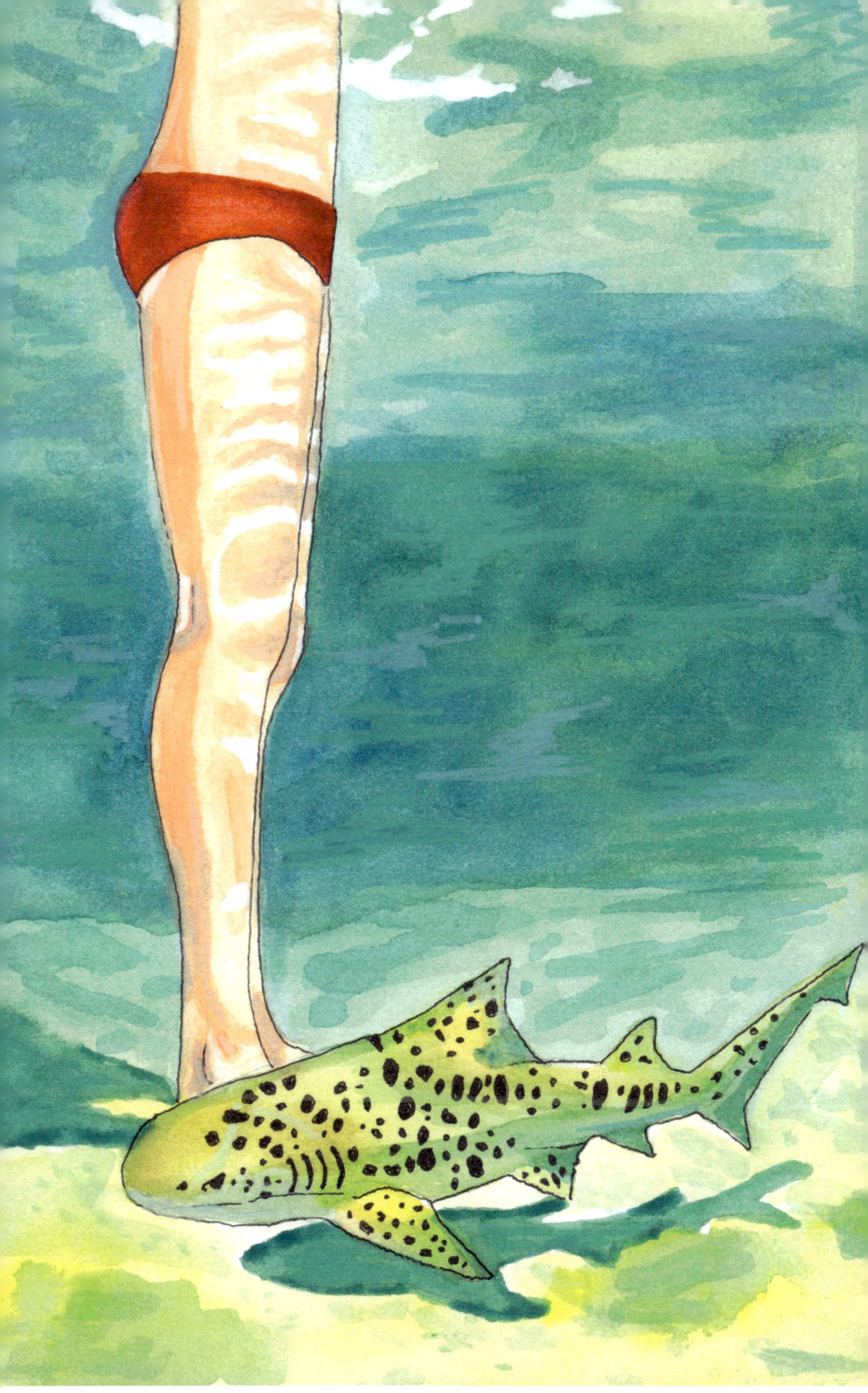

I have lived in the San Bernardino area my entire life and one of the great things we have is the Arrowhead.

The Arrowhead in the San Bernardino foothills is approximately 1,300 feet long and 450 feet wide, covering about 7.5 acres. This naturally occurring formation is clearly visible for miles due to the contrasting light soil on its face against the darker surrounding chaparral. Below where the Arrowhead points are natural springs. Arrowhead Springs, Lake Arrowhead and Arrowhead Avenue in San Bernardino are named after this great landmark.

Arrowhead Mountain
Colored pencil
Letter: A
C. Cotter

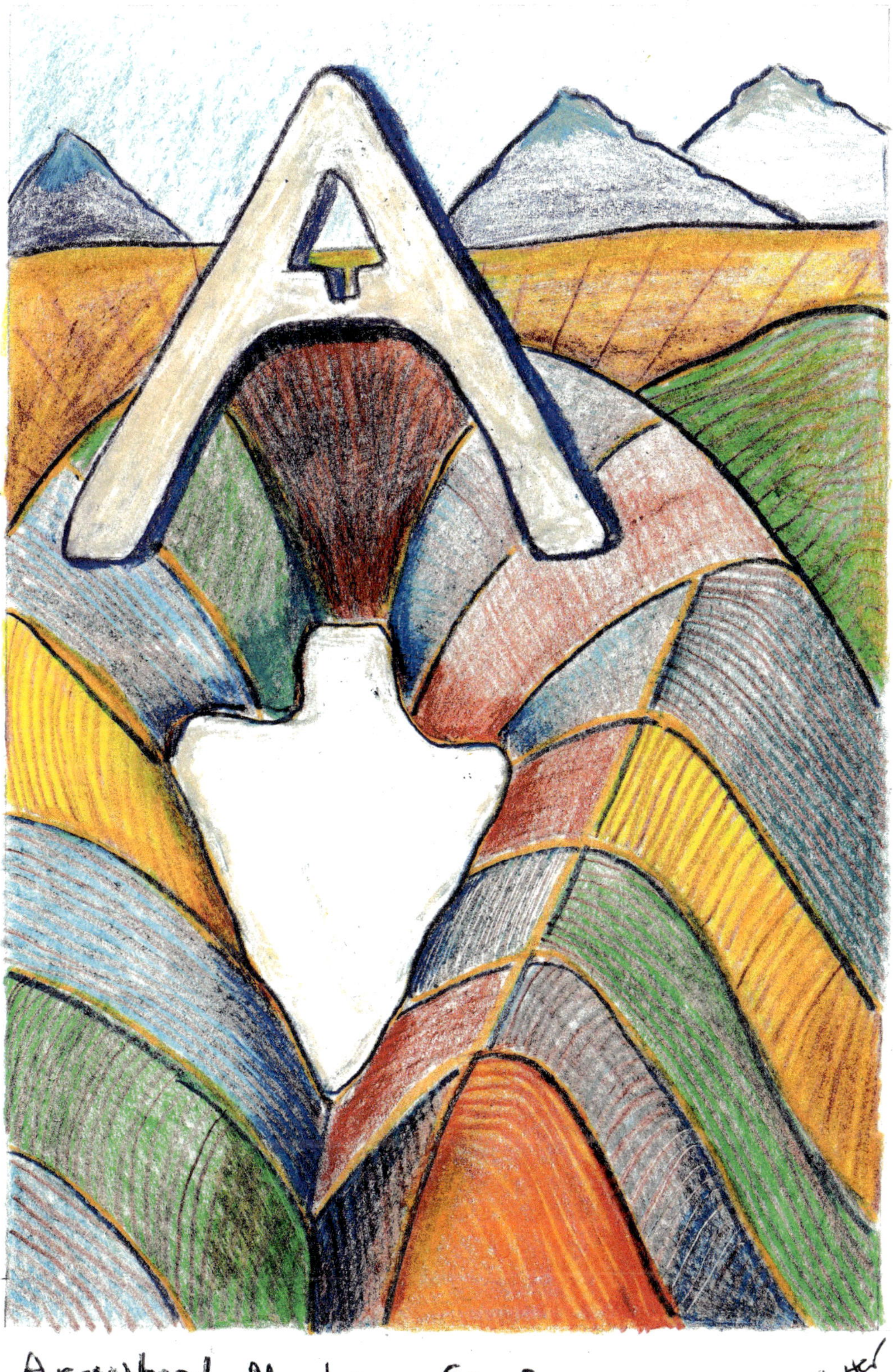

Arrowhead Mountain - San Bernardino, CA C. Cotter

This drawing shows how land, sea, and sky are connected through our state's native wildlife. These animals all live in different places but share the same state.

The rainbow forms the shape of an "N," which stands for natural beauty of California.

This artwork reminds us to appreciate and protect the beauty of our state.

The Spirit of California Nature

Digital

Letter: N

Charlie Schimmel

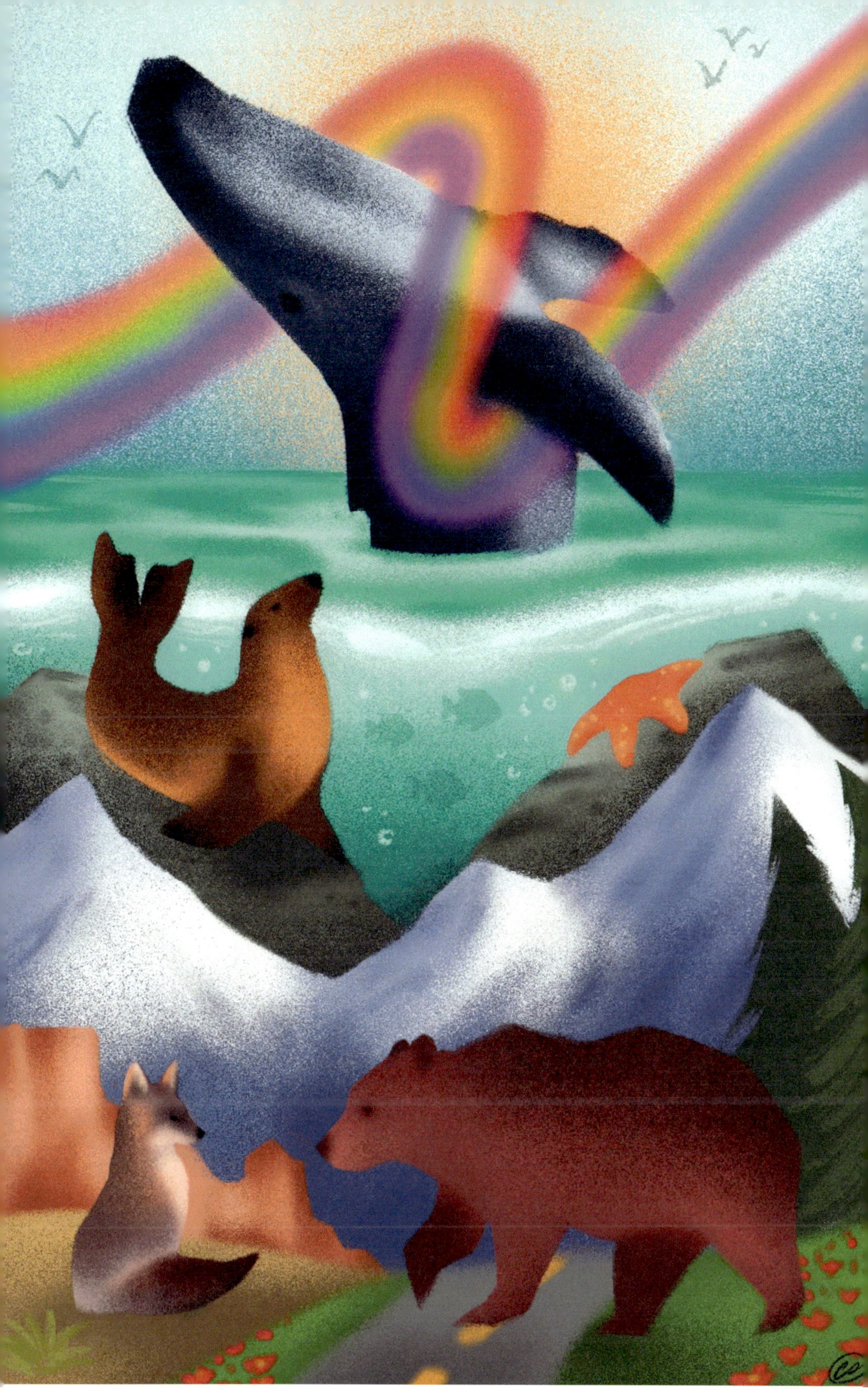

The first time I ever participated in one of California's famous Grunion runs was in college, late at night on the shore.
I was bad at catching the fish, so I'd wait for the tide to rush in and for all the grunions to wash up on the rocks for me to snatch them up. I remember how the beach would glitter with silver, and even in the height of night, the water wasn't too cold.

Like an old memory, I decided to draw this in a monochrome color scheme, evoking the quiet getaway of a midnight adventure.

Grunion Run
Digital
Letter: G
Amanda Le

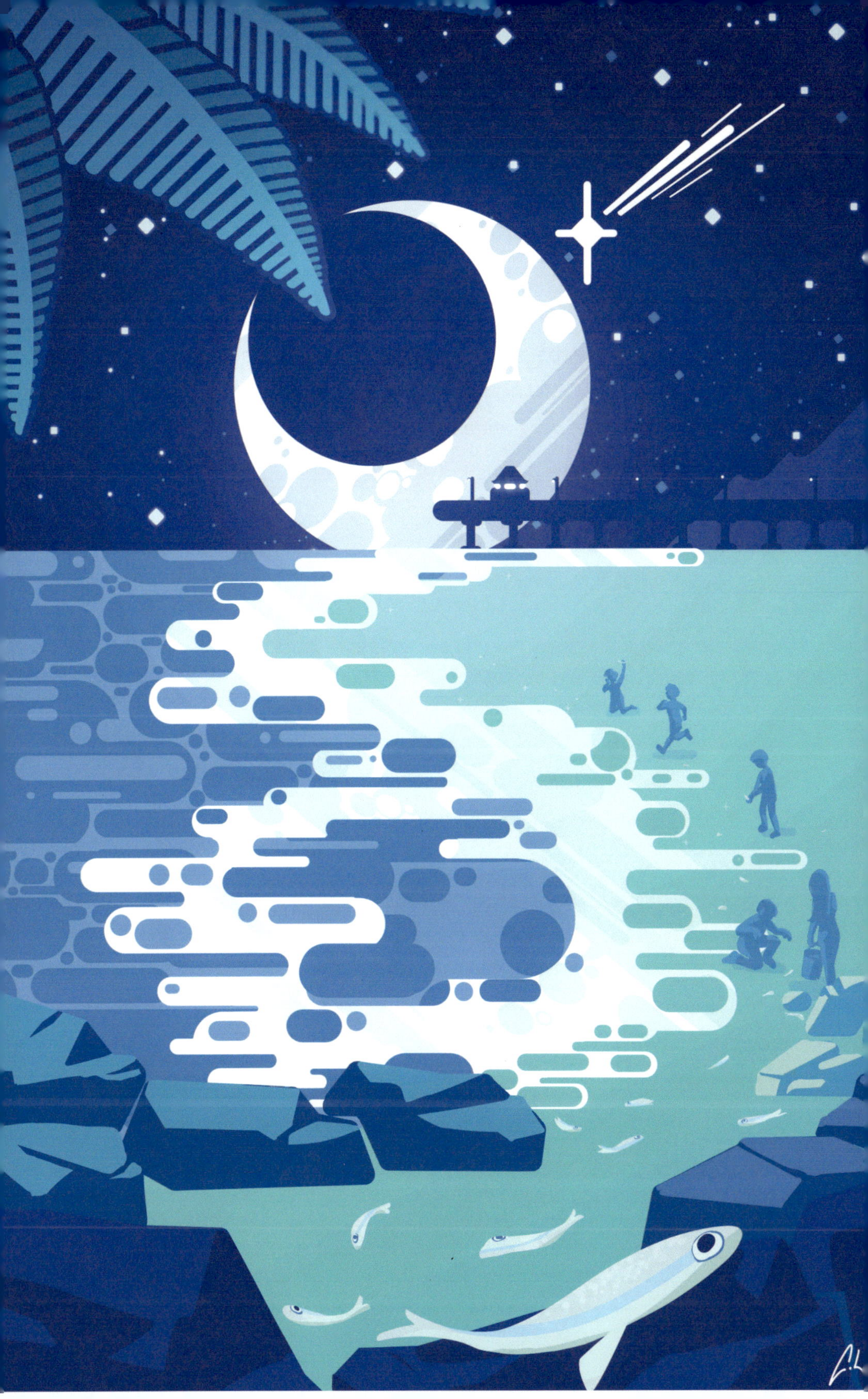

The "U" inspired the famous Golden Gate Bridge due to the inherent shape of the main cables. I have a lot of love for San Francisco for its LGBTQ historical significance, art scene, friends who live there, and my grandparents.

Go-Uh-lden Gate Bridge
Mixed Media (Pencil / Digital tablet + Photoshop)
Letter: U
Alex Kelly

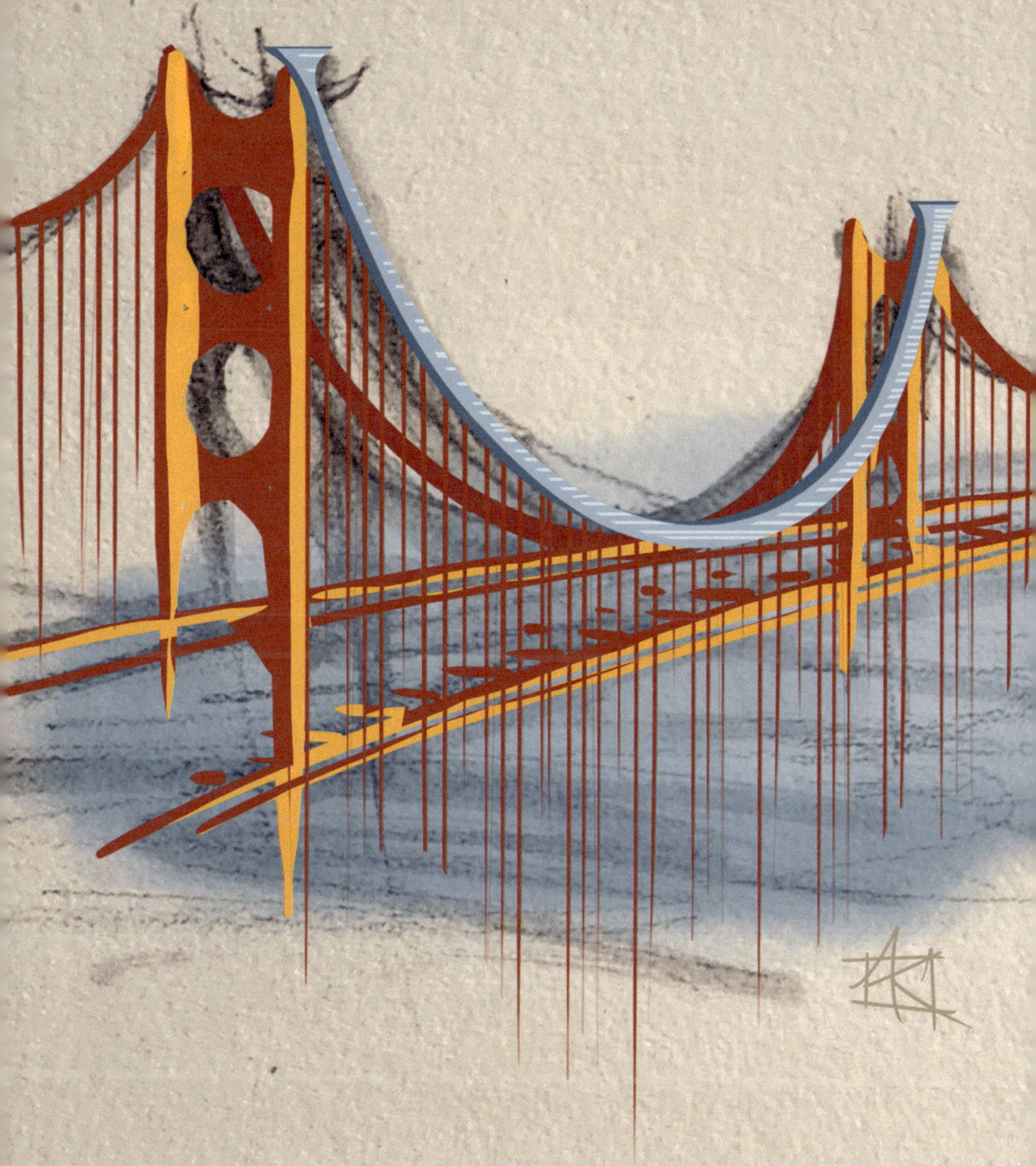

The California theme being presented is how diverse the ecosystem is with its animal inhabitants. The snake representing the many predators that, even if they can be hostile, live in the area and should be respected and given the honor and status they deserve. Alongside the snake, though appearing as against it, the person depicted shows how we should side with the natures of our home rather than push it away, with the fact that the weapon is art and creation rather than something deadly.

don't bite the hand that paints you

Digital Art

Letter: A

Z Morales

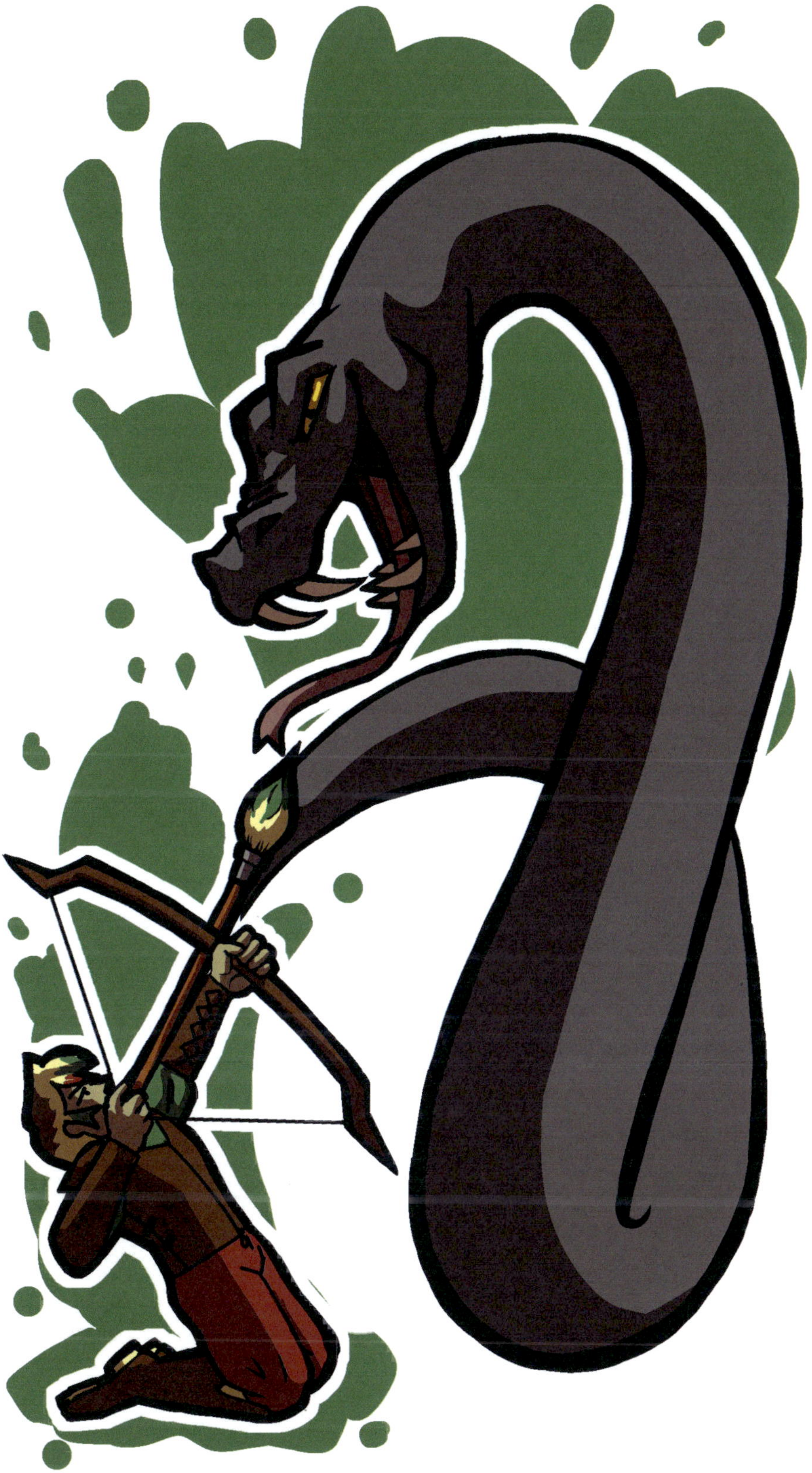

Of all the possible fish along the expansive California coast, how lucky are we to be able to claim the beautiful, golden Garibaldi as our State Fish. The contrast of their golden scales, swimming among the massive beds of deep green kelp is a beautiful sight to see. Something we Californians should never take for granted. It's always a joy to spot one!

Garibaldi
Digital Art / ProCreate
Letter: G
Tony Moramarco

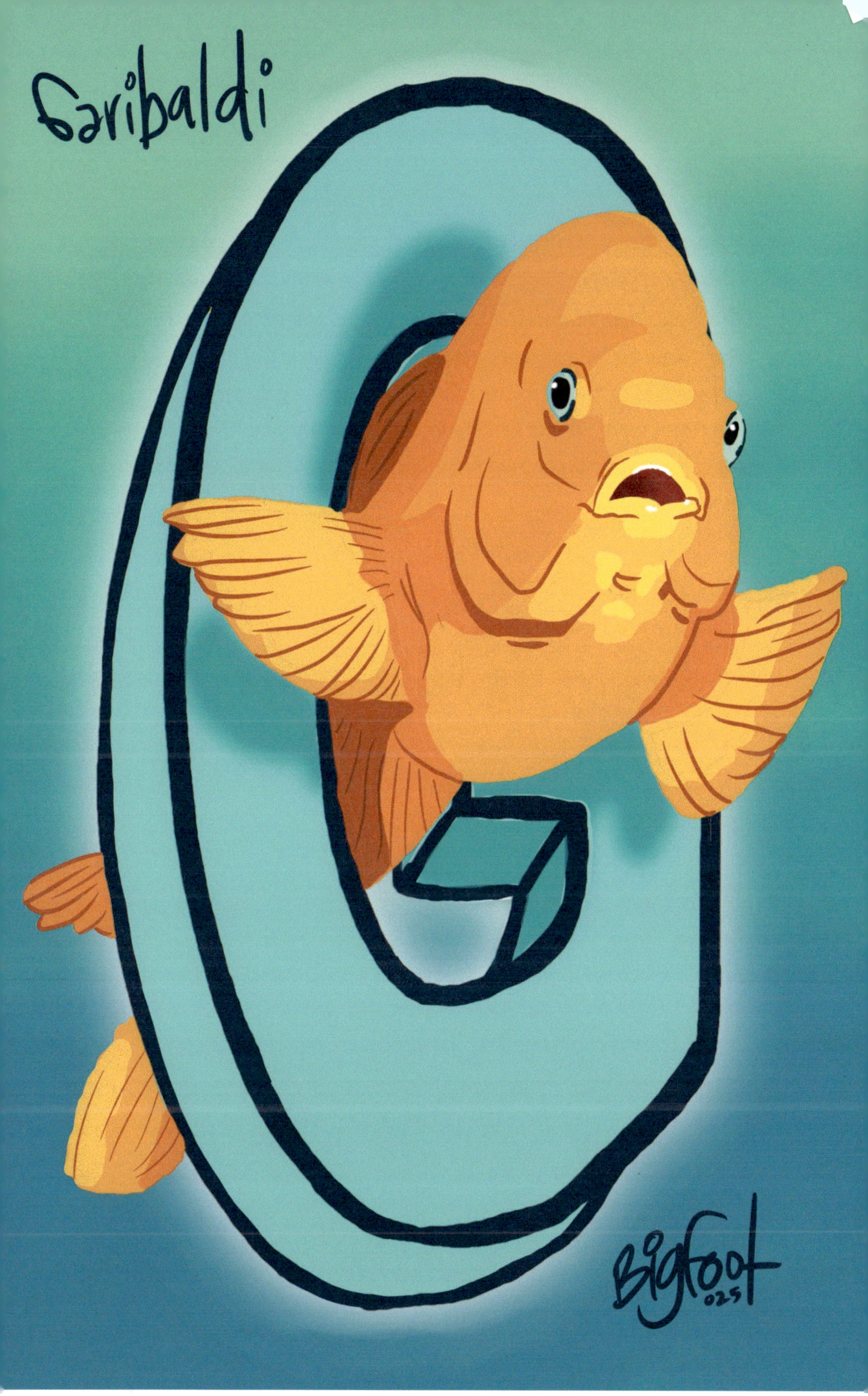
Garibaldi
Bigfoot
025

The Gold Rush is a well-known part of the state's history. The Great Seal of California adopted by the California Constitutional Convention of 1849 included the depiction of a gold miner, and the Greek word Eureka which means "I have found it." Thus, it is fitting to include an homage to the state's motto for a California theme.

Eureka
Watercolor and pen
Letter: E
Robin Wesley

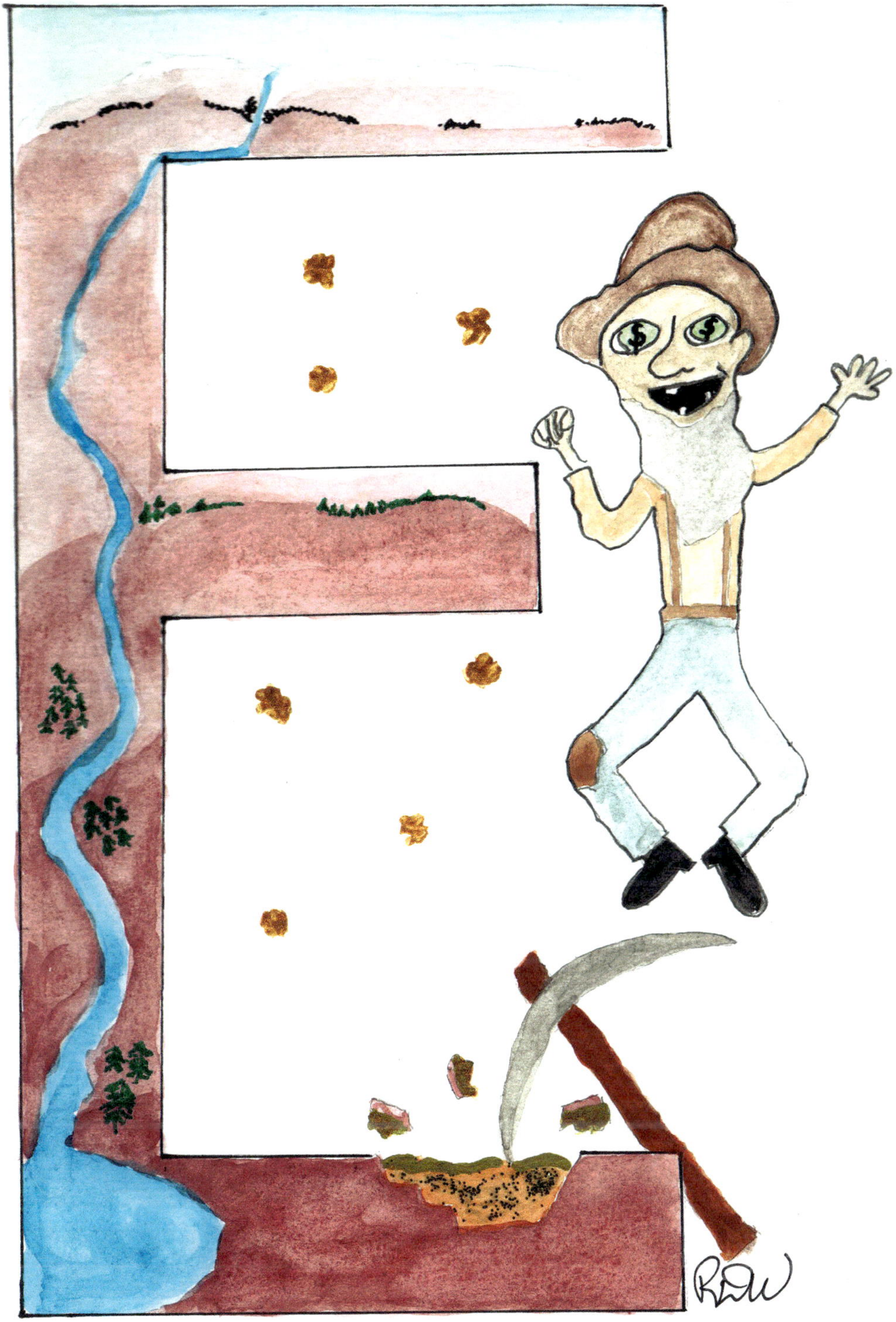

I chose to do a piece based on the ocean and the wildlife that inhabit the waters, including the yellowfin tuna, orca whale, bottle nose dolphin, California moray eel, and garibaldi. Wildlife is extremely important, not only to us as humans, but also to the ecosystem and the planet.

I hope my piece inspires people to think about the oceans and how they make up 70% of the Earth we inhabit.

Protect Our Ocean Friends
Graphite and coloured pencil with watercolor paint
Letter: O
Sabin R. Flores

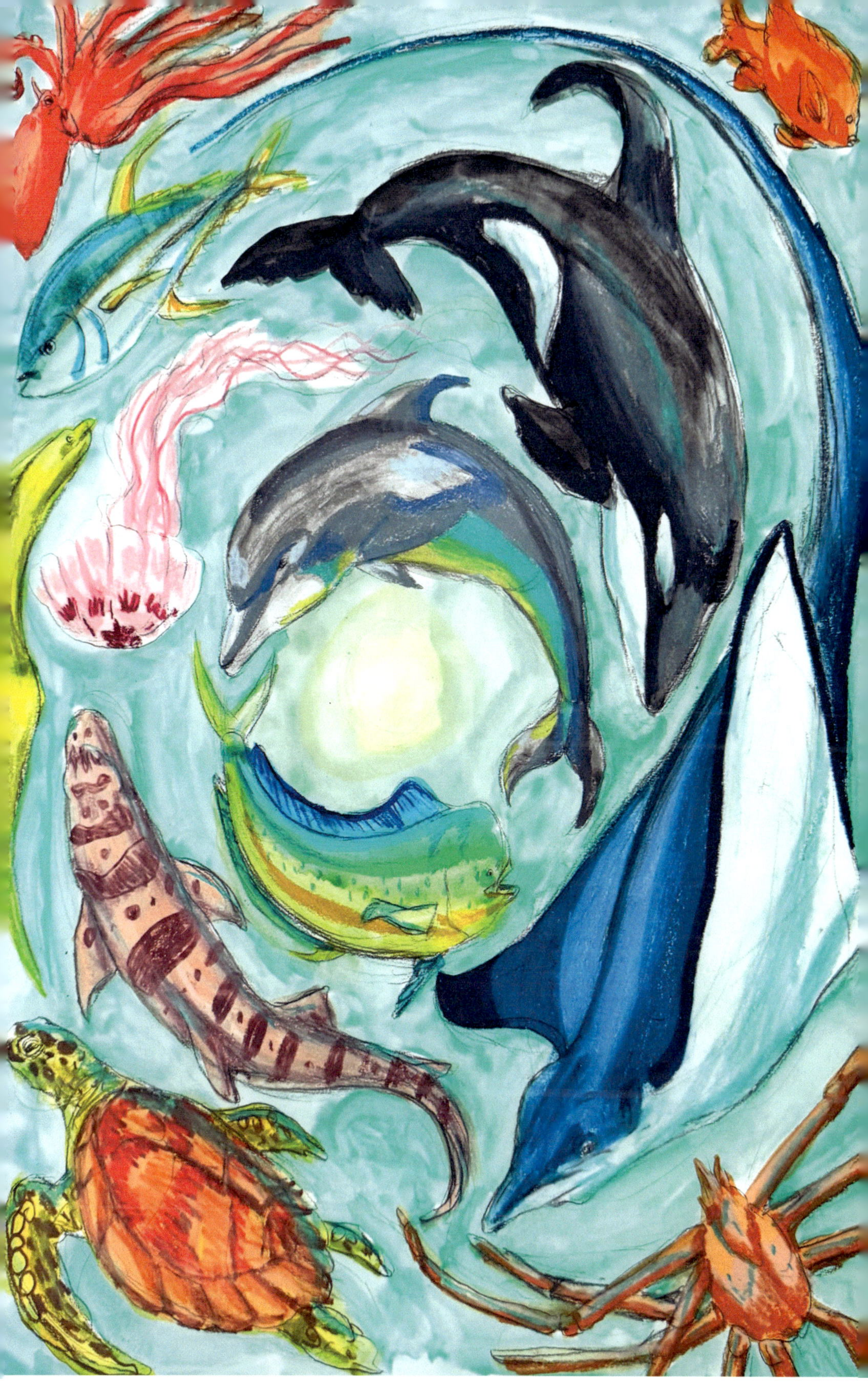

Anyone who lives in California or visits knows the extent to which freeways allow for mobility. Public transportation is limited or absent in various parts of the state. We mainly rely on cars, buses and trucks to get from one point to another, or even to enter or exit the state. Californians generally know the hours the freeways they use are congested with traffic and the times they are not. Despite the nuisance of stalled vehicles, the danger of possible accidents, obstacles in the road. and times of maintenance or construction, California freeways are essential and certainly should be appreciated.

The Freeways of California

Digital Art

Letter: F

Robert Lewis Rieger

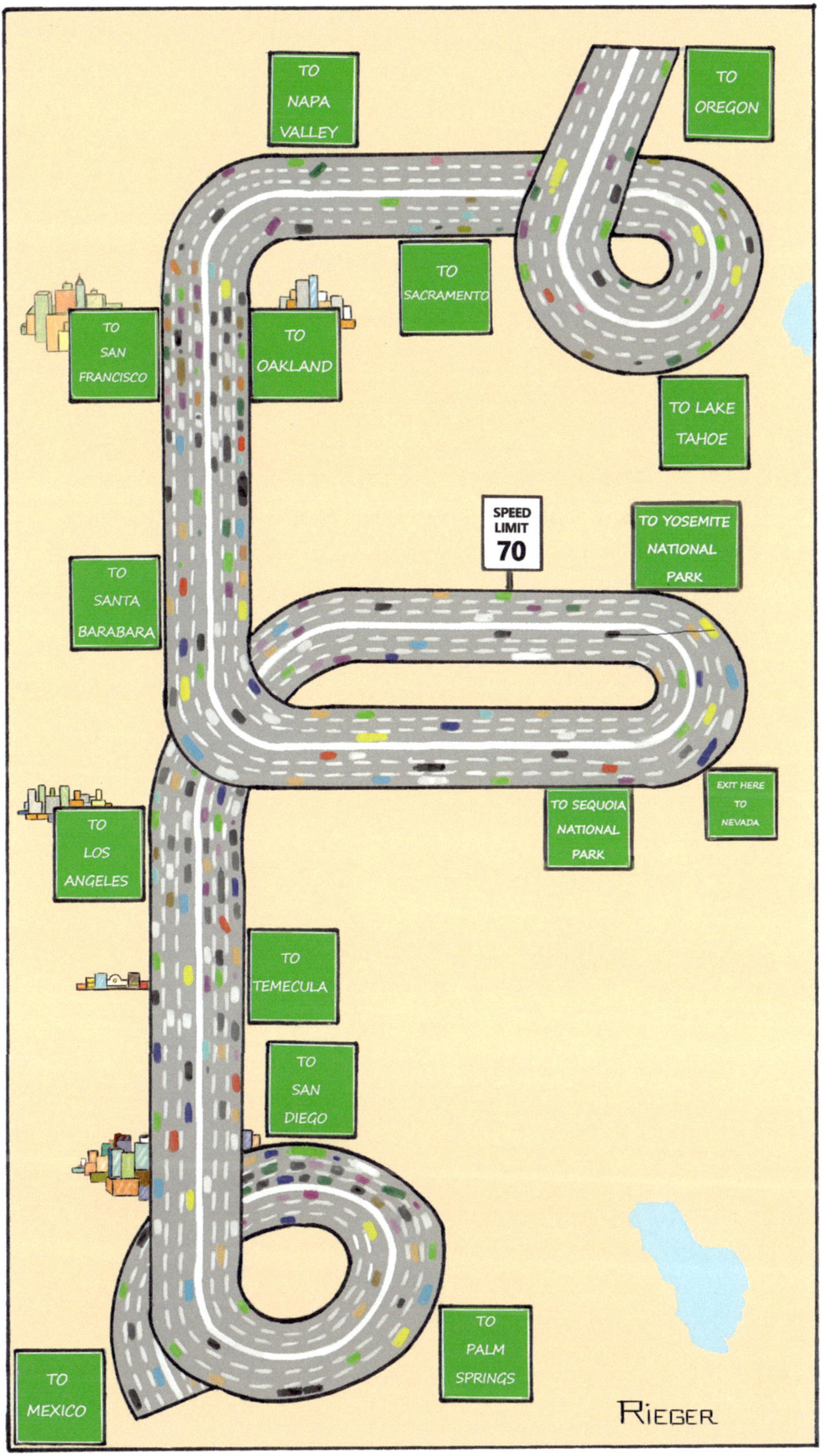

TO NAPA VALLEY
TO OREGON
TO SACRAMENTO
TO SAN FRANCISCO
TO OAKLAND
TO LAKE TAHOE
SPEED LIMIT 70
TO YOSEMITE NATIONAL PARK
TO SANTA BARABARA
TO LOS ANGELES
TO SEQUOIA NATIONAL PARK
EXIT HERE TO NEVADA
TO TEMECULA
TO SAN DIEGO
TO PALM SPRINGS
TO MEXICO
RIEGER

Like all other states in the USA, California has its own Wonderlands to visit. Joshua Tree National Park is one of them, located In Southern California.

Due to Pasadena resident Minerva Hoyt's efforts to preserve this land, President Franklin D. Roosevelt declared it a National Monument in 1936. Located in Mohave Desert, these unique trees protect the land in harsh climate. The rock formations are amazing too. People go overnight camping to stargaze in the absolute darkness.

Joshua Tree
Color pencils
Letter: T
Kausar P Malik

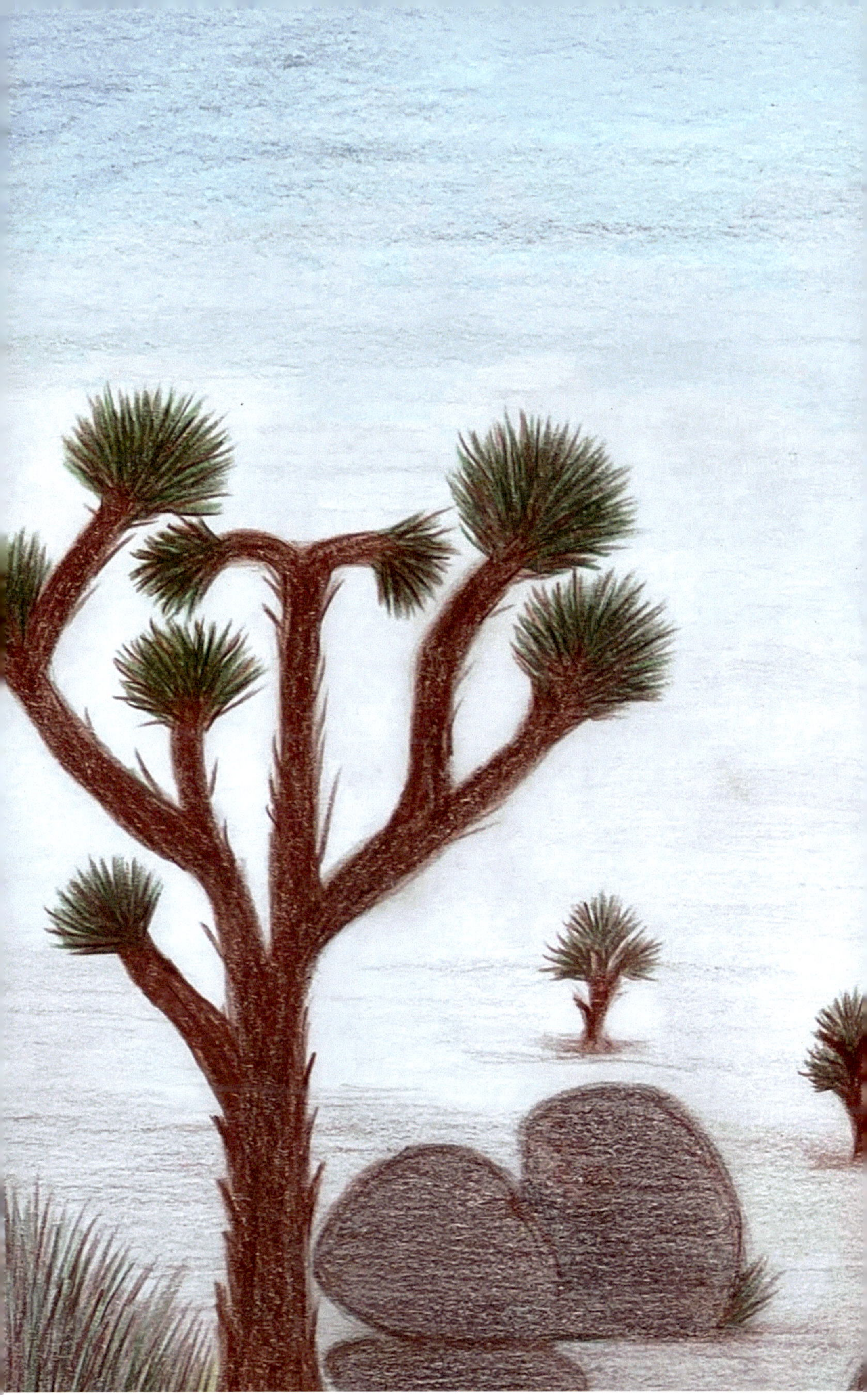

I love California history and the old Hotel Del Coronado takes me to another place and time. Grand Victorian architecture, ghost stories, golden-age Hollywood celebrities, iconic authors, and beautiful beaches conjure to make it one of my favorite California places to escape to and create. Besides, our oldest son was married on the beach at the Hotel Del, so I had to make it the choice to illustrate this letter.

Hotel Del Coronado, My Hotel California

Acrylic, Gouache

Letter: H

Bonnie Martland

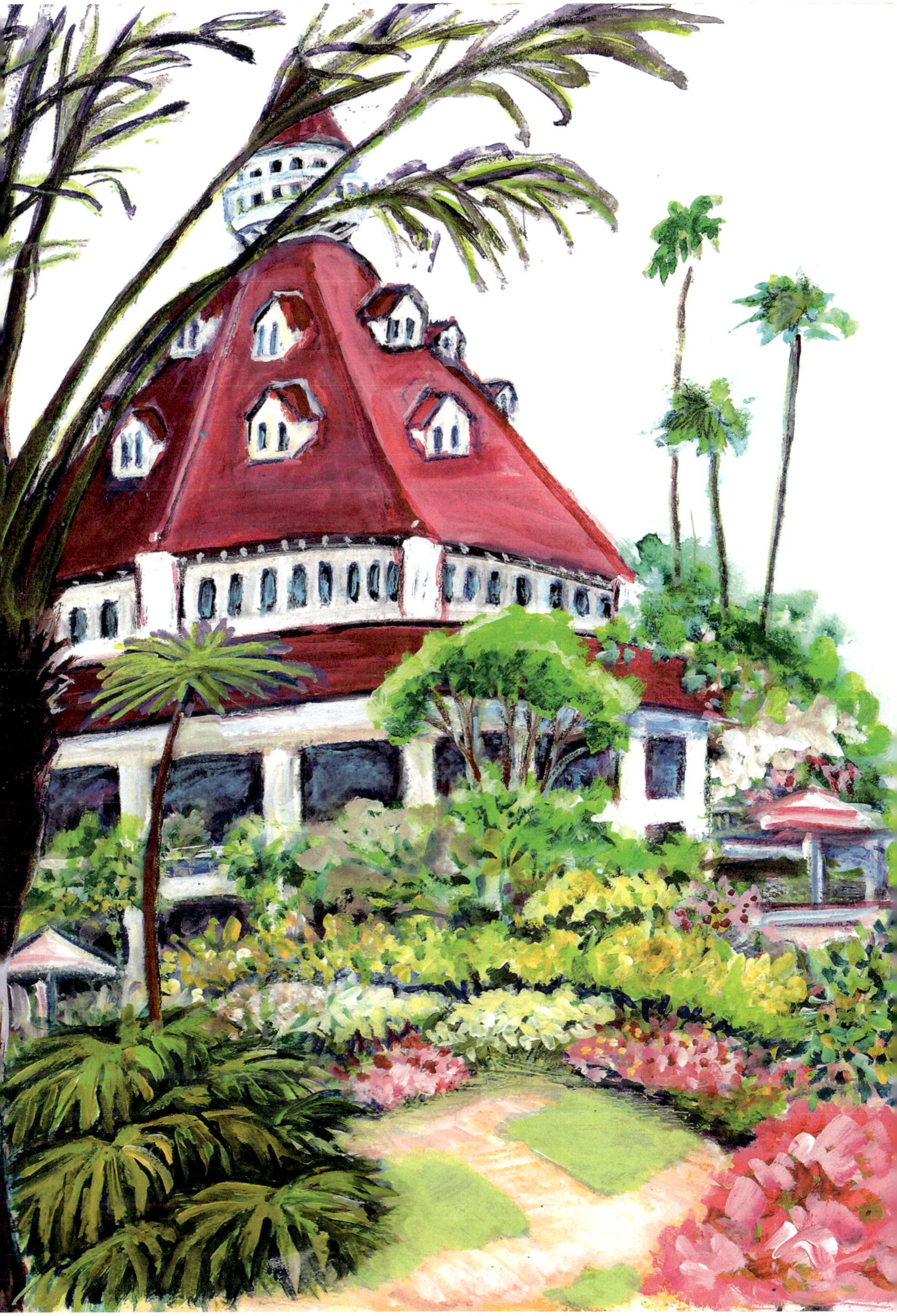

Growing up a vineyard kid in Temecula's Wine Country was an unknown privilege for me. My father, John Moramarco being one of Temecula's Wine Country Pioneers, I spent much of my youth out in the vineyards, or somewhere in or near a winery.

I was oblivious to how unique and wonderful that was. All I wanted to do was draw and look at comic books. This design harkens back to that chapter of my life.

Wine Country
Digital Art / ProCreate
Letter: E
Tony Moramarco

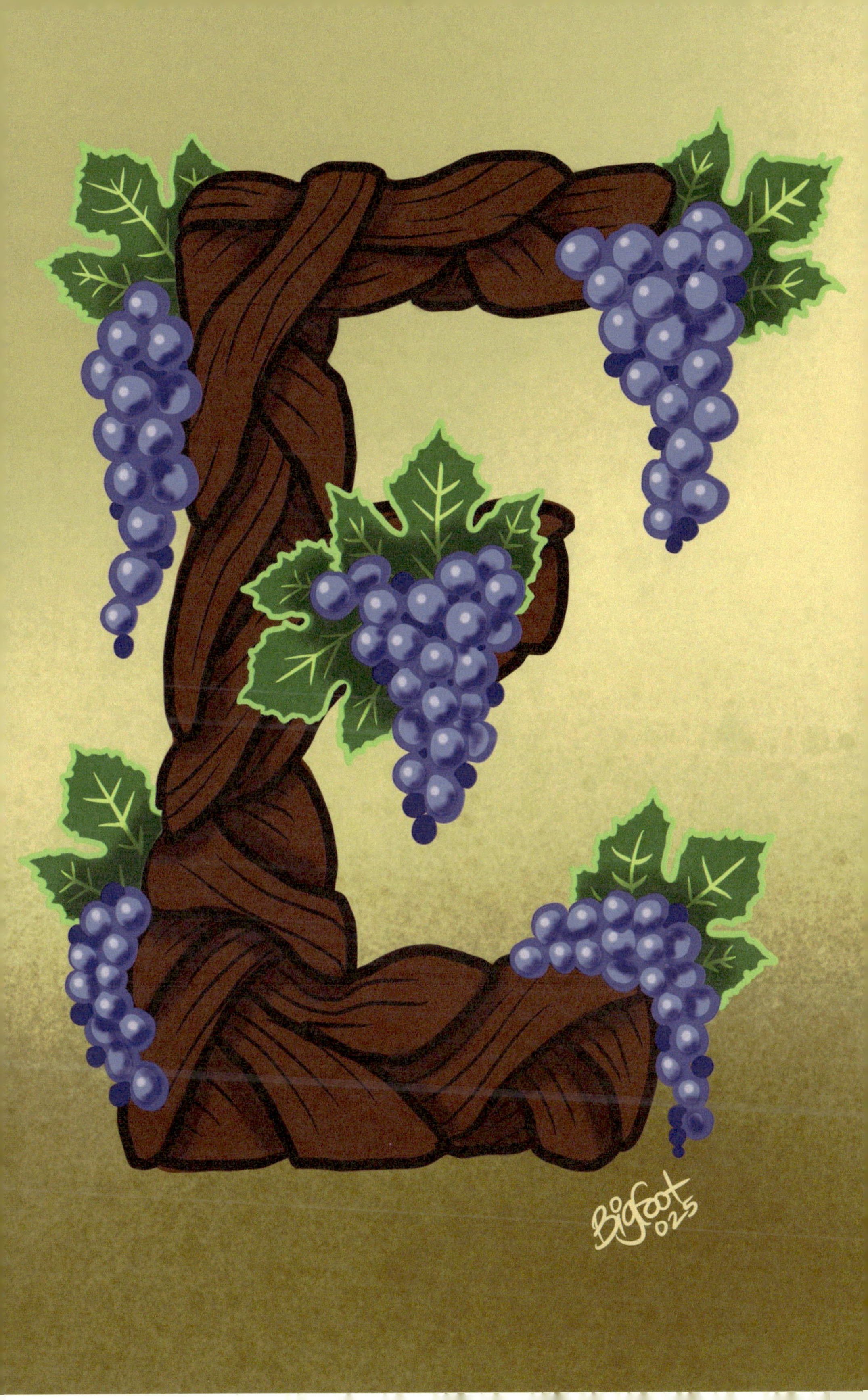
Bigfoot
025

While I was growing up in Southern California, my family would go hiking from time to time in the San Gabriel Mountains. I also attended summer and winter camps in the San Bernardino Mountain Range. These excursions to the mountains fostered my love of forests and spending time in nature. California is home to different kinds of ecosystems, forests, plant life, and wildlife. While I've been blessed to experience all the wonder and beauty there is across this state, the forests of So-Cal hold a special place in my heart.

For this art piece, I was inspired by the special occasions where my family would go hiking in the snow. It was always so magical walking into this quiet wintry world and seeing the glistening snow covering the tree branches and the ground. It's an experience that I sought to capture in this drawing. This illustration is based on a picture I took while hiking with my family on Mt. Baldy in the wintertime. Although I did not see a black bear when I was there that day, I included one to represent one of the native animals that live in and roam the California mountains. This drawing is an homage to the snowy quaint forests of California that are often forgotten in the sunny state.

Snowfall in Mt. Baldy
Digital
Letter: F
Kimberley Cornell

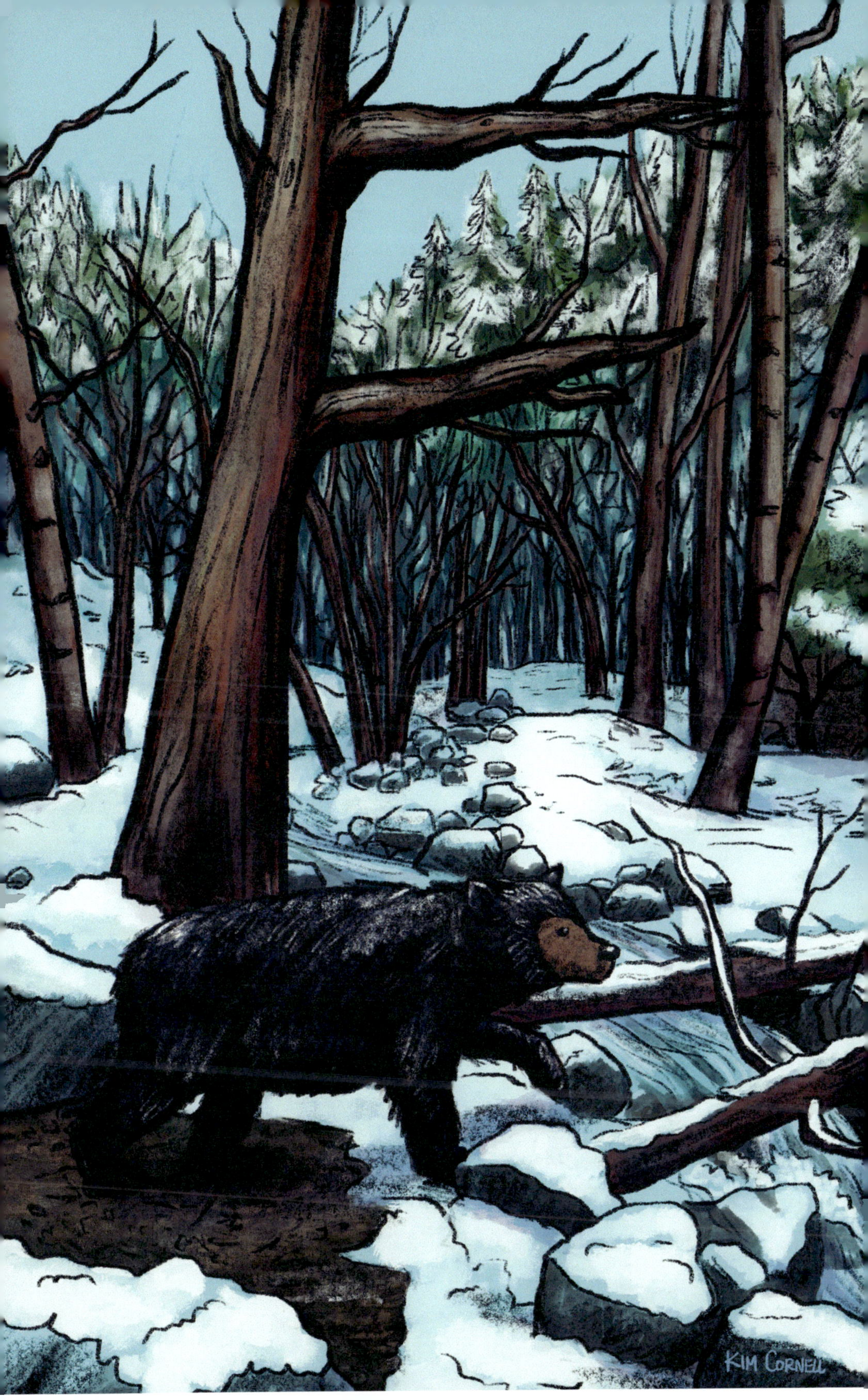
KIM CORNELL

California is one of the most desirable travel locations.

In Southern California, when we look to the sky, mostly it is blue and full of sunshine. Yet there, mixed with the morning marine layer, is a sky covered in contrails from airplanes.

When I observe this, I am reminded that in many places around the world they don't see these kinds of fuel trails from airplanes, but from missiles.

Blue Skies Ahead
Acrylic on 12x18 Cotton Canvas
Letter: E
Sacha Hope

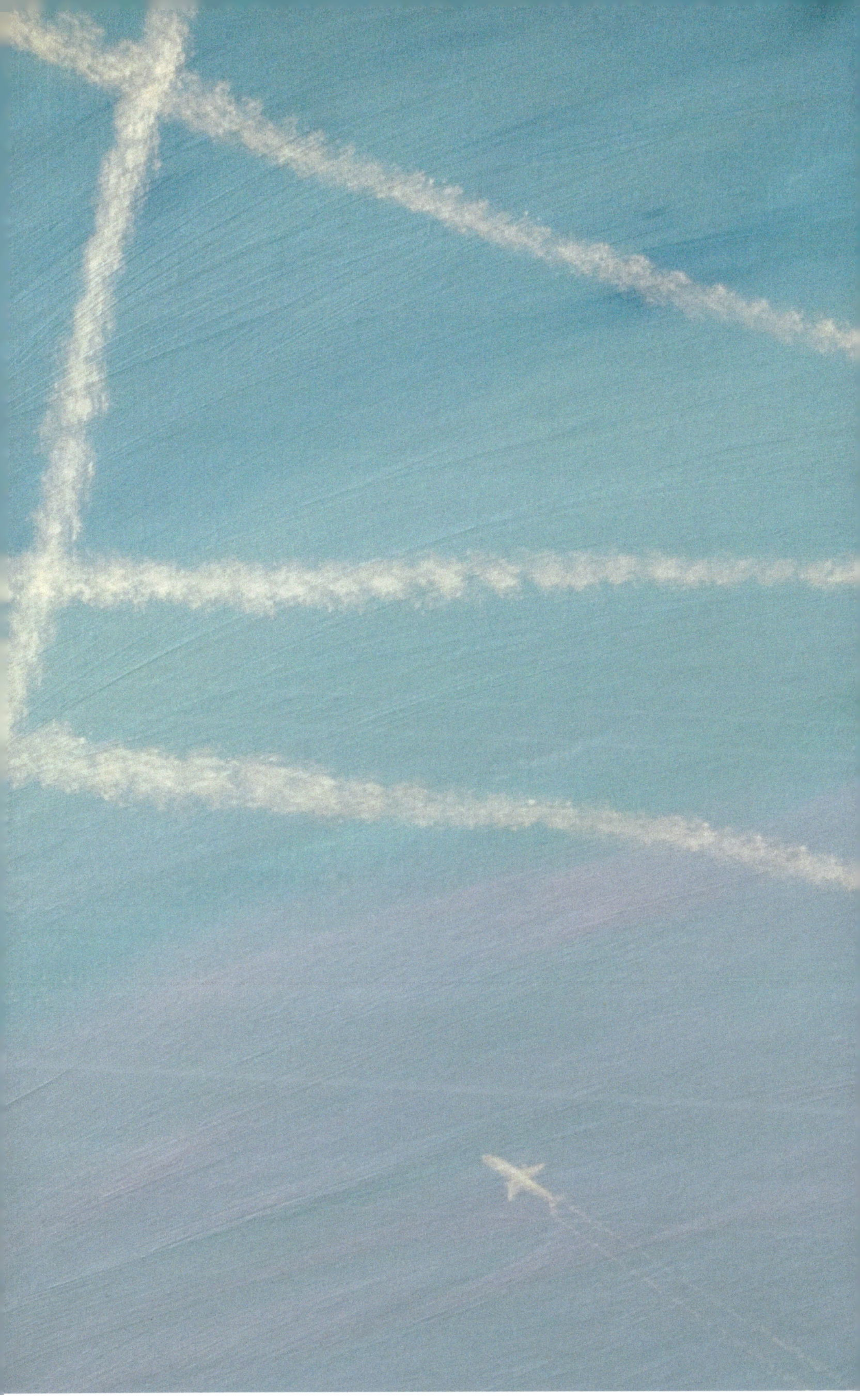

This plein air painting was created in Barrio Logan, only a block away from Chicano Park and the Coronado Bridge.

The murals I found in this alley reflect the mass amount of Chicano art around this colorful neighborhood. It shows that art and culture live even in the lesser seen parts of our communities: in alleys and under bridges. I love art the most when I find it in unlikely places, where you know the artist did it for the love of creating. Keep expressing yourself!

Callejón
Digital Paint, Procreate
Letter: A
Adam Favela

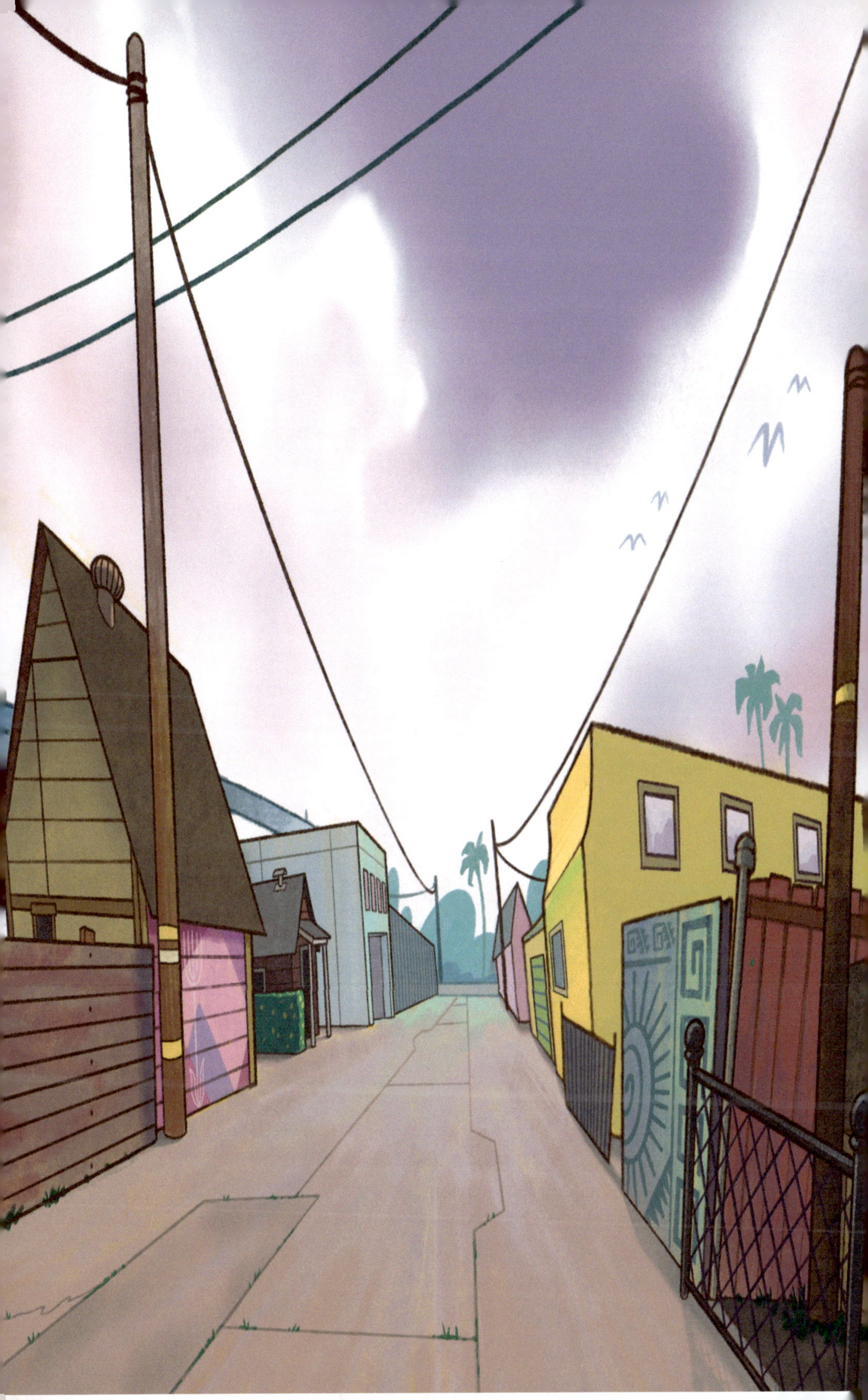

“Held Against Time” is about slowness, endurance, and the quiet strength found in nature. Inspired by California’s redwood trees, this piece reflects how it feels to stand next to something ancient and unbothered. It invites you to slow down, feel and sit with time instead of rushing through it.

Held Against Time
Digital Art (Procreate/Adobe Photoshop)
Letter: R
Brooke Olson

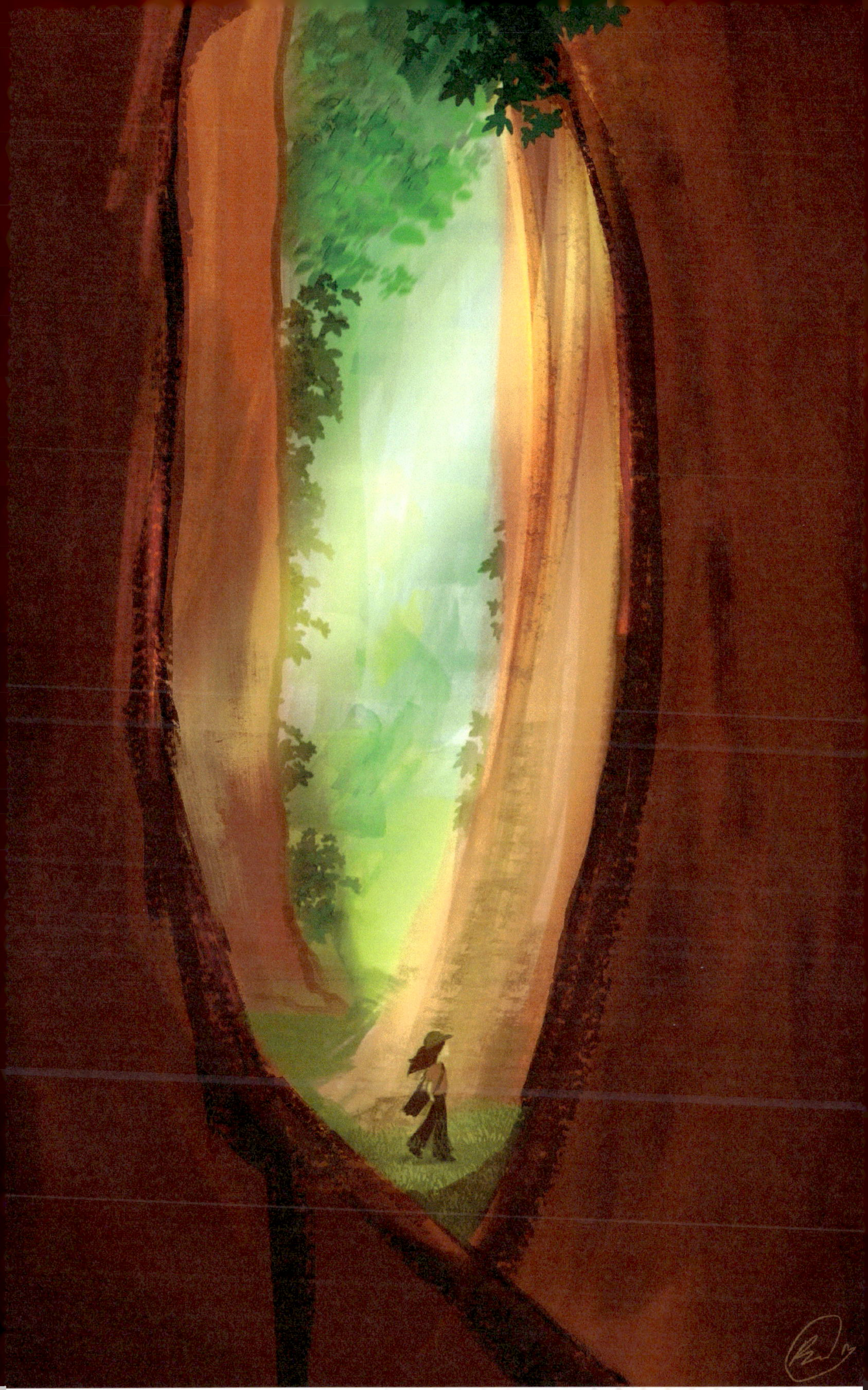

Little tiny dinosaurs live in our Southern California yards ... eating bugs and greeting us on warm, sunny mornings. Their little heads flip around, trying to stay aware of everything around them. They are also push-up champions! If you ever move to a place where there are no tiny dinosaurs, you better believe you will miss them!

Lizards
Digital Art / ProCreate
Letter: L
Tony Moramarco

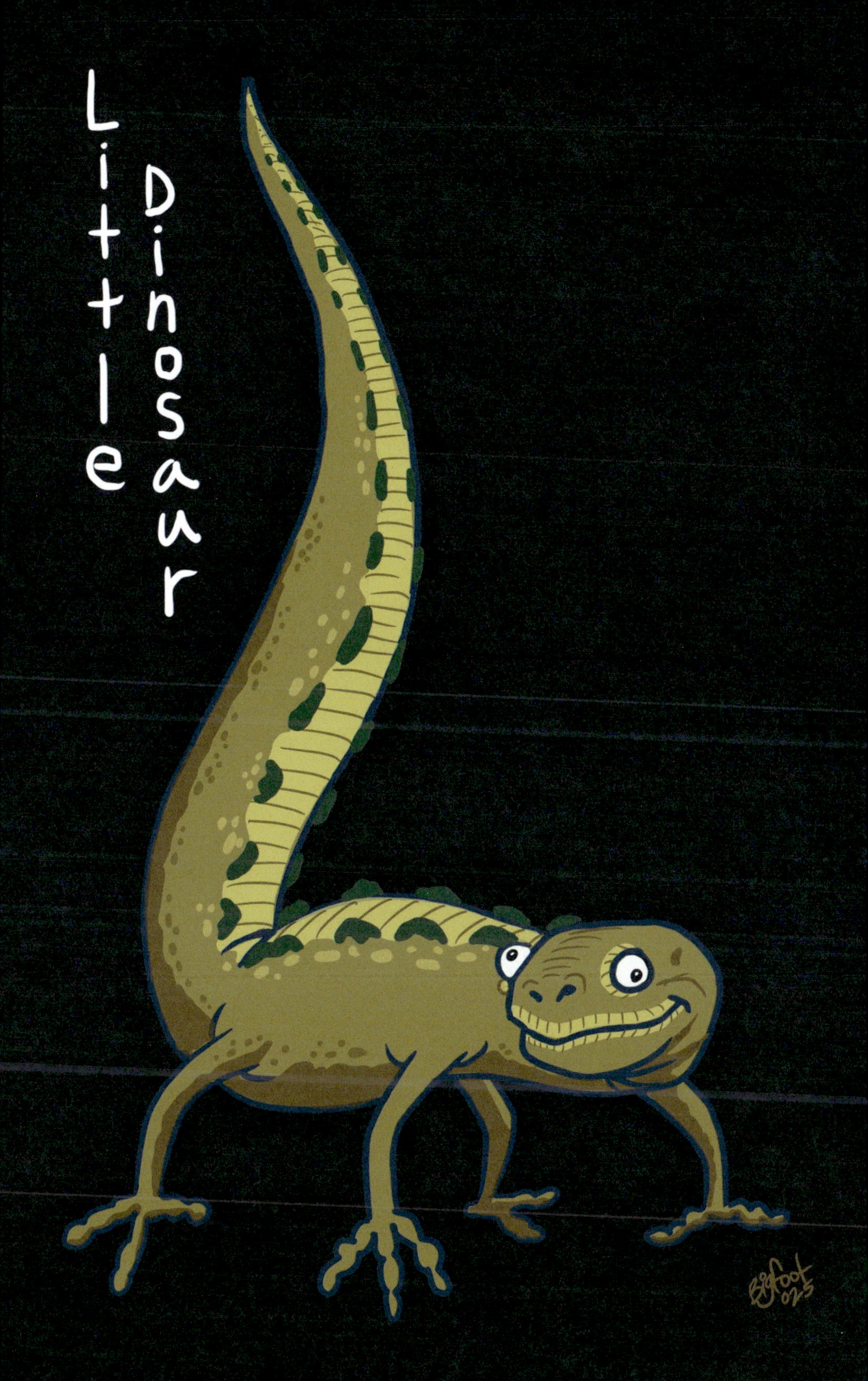
Little
Dinosaur

Lounging under a damp morning sky, Elephant Seals fill the beach at the Piedras Blancas Rookery.

Piedras Blancas is the only elephant seal rookery in the world that is easily accessible and open to the public every day of the year, and it's just a few miles north of San Simeon, CA, gateway to Hearst Castle.

Elephant Seals
Digital Drawing on Sketchbook Pro for iPad
Letter: E
John Waddleton

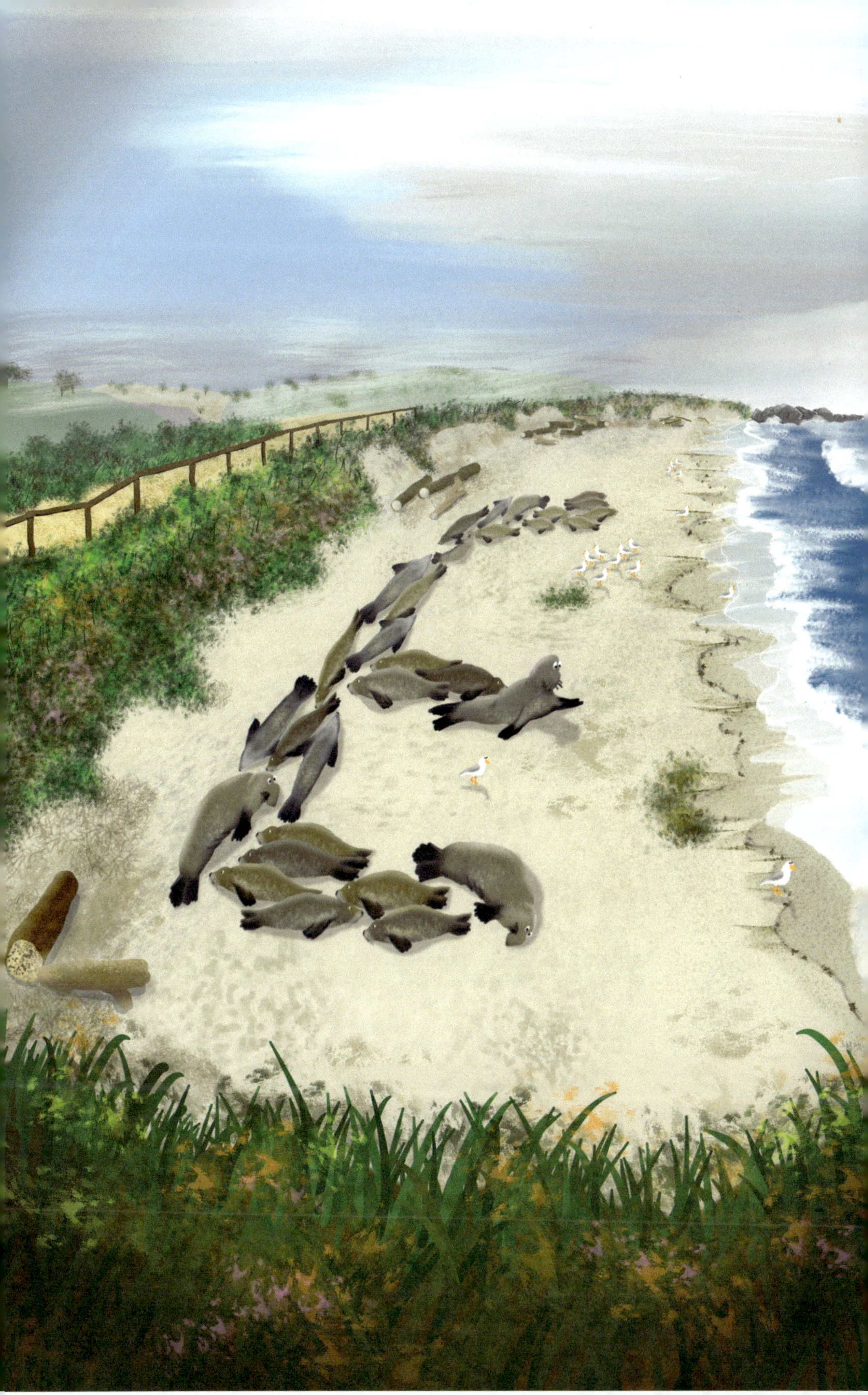

A kid makes a castle with shovel and sand.
"All of the world shall now understand!
I am the King of this salty, wet land!"
He proclaims to the beach, green pail in his hand.

A white-capping wave rumbles and curls,
crashes, retreats, disappearing his world.
He knows how waves work...kinda, but then,
the trickier part is the where and the when.
"Oh well," says the kid. "I'll just build it again!"

"S"
Colored pencil/ink
Letter: S
Michael Smith

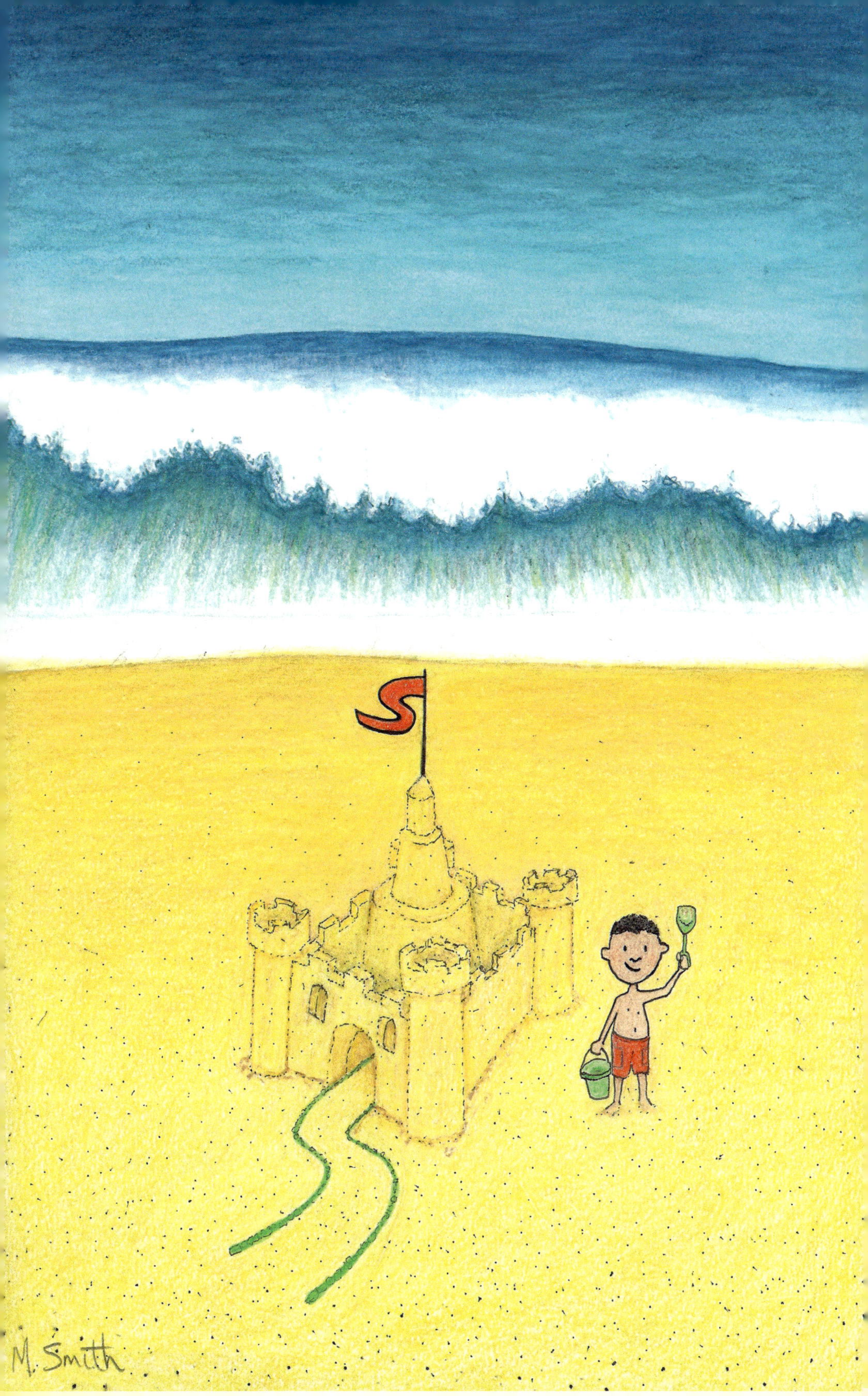
M. Smith

The California Sea Lion (Zalophus californianus) is the first animal that comes to mind when I think about our beautiful coasts. Their loud barks permeate the shore, inviting many locals and tourists to gaze as they play and bask in the sun. They are a symbol of the most biodiverse state in the country. The health and population of sea lions help us better understand how California's ecosystem is doing. This art piece represents the sea lion's importance of the health of California's coast.

California's Star

Digital

Letter: S

Alex

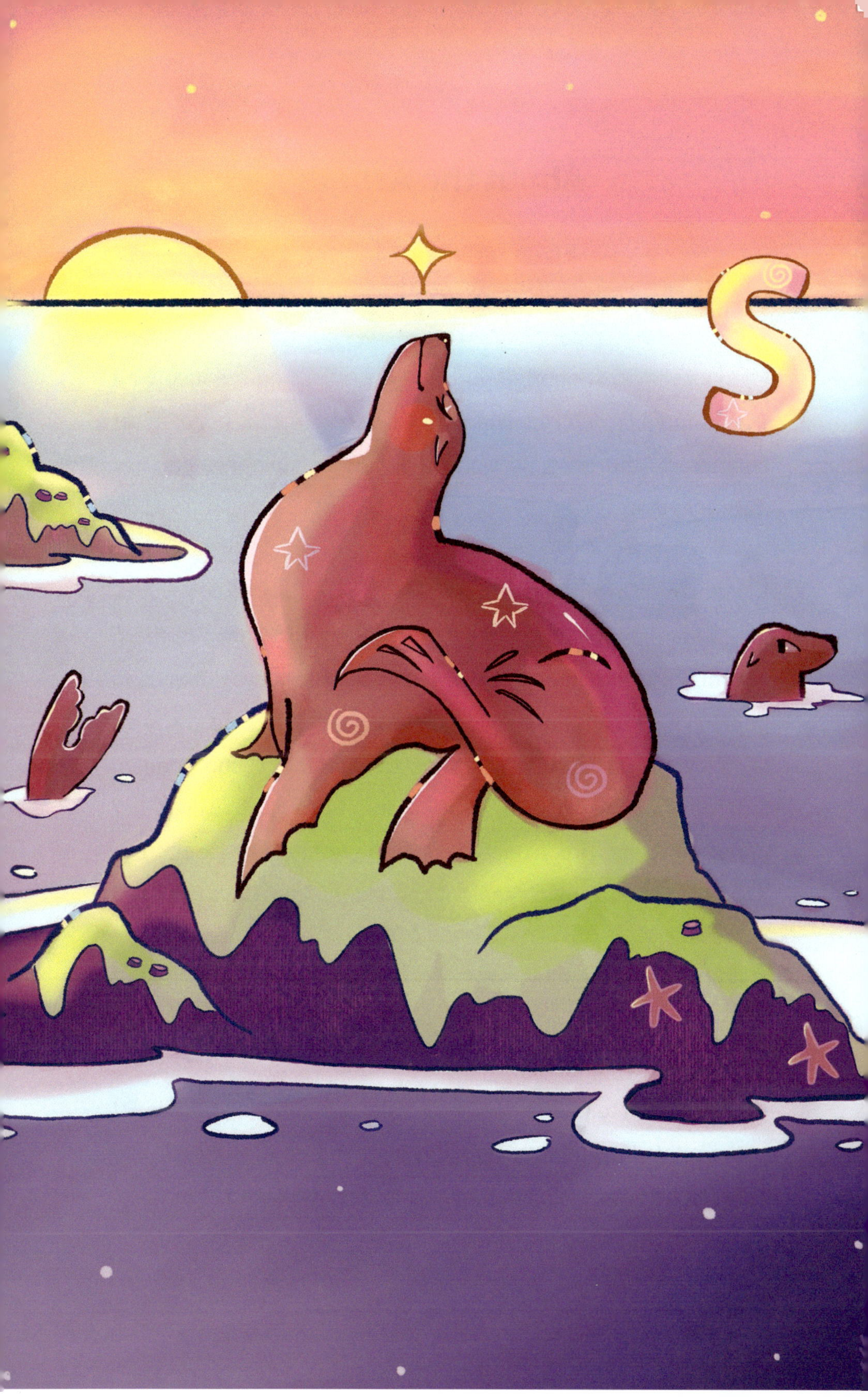
S

About the Artists

Alex

My name is Alex, she/her, and I'm an artist and creative who enjoys making colorful and fun art. Most of that consists of characters and animals done digitally, by painting, clay, or mixed media.

Kimberley Cornell

Kimberley Cornell is an artist and illustrator from Southern California. The themes of her artwork are primarily whimsy and nostalgia, with a little humor. Her love for storytelling is shown in her work through her creation of characters and scenes. Kimberley enjoys working in a variety of media, however, her current favorites are ink and digital. She tends to be inspired by people, movies, music, fashion, and stories from days gone by.

C.Cotter

C.Cotter is a native of the San Bernardino area and worked in education as his first career. Since retiring two years ago, his goal has been to learn various forms of art including traditional and digital drawing and painting with the goal of illustrating children's books. Using colored pencils, "Arrowhead Mountain" is his first published drawing.

Adam Favela

Adam is an Illustrator and Designer from Temecula, California. He loves plein air painting, background design for animation, photography, and graphic design for public spaces. He is most inspired by vibrant colors and the visual identities of skateboarding culture and Latin-American art, popularly found in Southern California.

Sabin R. Flores

Sabin is an artist and art teacher that resides in Southern California. They specialize in mixed media work and a variety of different art forms including, acrylic painting, traditional drawing, watercolor, and crocheting. Catch them constantly creating @anonymous.__.weirdo on Instagram.

Tiara Harvey

Tiara Harvey is a multidisciplinary artist and designer best known for blending craftsmanship, whimsy, and precision. Her work balances playfulness with intention, influenced by design history and thoughtful minimalism. Her submitted piece reflects her love of atmosphere, detail, and creating art that feels both personal and inviting.

Sacha Hope

Award-winning Artist Sacha Hope is best known for her bright, cheerful and vibrant paintings. A British-born transplant to the USA, Sacha currently resides in the rural high desert of Southern

California. A functional artist inspired by nature, current events and humans, her writing is lyrical, short and often full of profanities.

“I write to cleanse my mind. I paint, because it lets the sun shine through me!” Find her art at **www.SachaHope.com**.

Amy Huffmire

Amy Huffmire is a California-based artist and writer. A mother of five, she finds creative inspiration in the beauty of everyday moments. Her work draws from nature while exploring feelings and impressions, creating pieces that invite emotional connection and reflection. She writes in fiction, fantasy, and wellness, aiming to uplift and bring joy to the world around her.

Katinka

Katinka is a professional teaching artist who shows regularly throughout California. She is obsessed with color and has traveled extensively to study Van Gogh and the French Boheme artists. She works mainly in painting, from acrylic, to oil, to watercolor and pastels, but always with bold color and often with humor. Her passion is inspiring creativity and helping others fulfill their creative potential.

Alex Kelly

Alex is a professional creative of currently fifteen years. Primarily working in mobile gaming creative strategy, she never hesitates when TVWI has an opportunity to draw, paint, or write. On the side, Alex might be caught on stage at a local Improv show or teaching a Paint and Sip class. She prioritizes time with friends and family and will often play D&D, run around a Ren Faire, and play board games or video games.

Stephenie Bushra Khan

Stephenie Bushra Khan is from Winchendon Massachusetts. Graduate of the School of Worcester Art Museum and a freelance writer, artist and poet, Stephenie has published both writing and art, nationally and internationally, in newspapers, online galleries, and magazines such as "Tiferet" and "Exposed Brick."

Amanda Le

Amanda Le is an award-winning Vietnamese-American artist born and raised in Southern California. They are proud to represent the LGBTQ+ community in literature as a nonbinary and bisexual artist. Their art focuses on their lived experiences, whimsical designs, and cute animals. When they're not creating art, they are teaching it to creatives of all ages.

Amanda designed a BIBA Award-winning book cover for poetry anthology *A Burning Lake of Paper Suns* by Ellen Webre, and became a book illustrator in 2023.

Kausar P Malik

Kausar P Malik resides in Temecula, California. She is a member of Temecula Valley Writers and Illustrators and an Associate Artist at Dorland Mountain Arts.

Brian Manning

Brian Manning. Local art instructor, freelance cartoonist, and all around swell fellow.

Elizabeth Weimer Marshall

For the past nineteen years, I served as a High School Spanish teacher, sharing not only language but also the beauty of Spanish culture. After retiring in 2024, I turned my full attention to creating art of my own—both functional pieces and purely expressive works. Every project begins with a drawing, grows into a sculpture, and is brought to life through color, texture, and form. I strive to blend my memories, imagination, and joy.

Bonnie Martland

A retired art teacher, Bonnie is a local artist with long ties to the Temecula Valley. Her art has been commissioned by the City of Temecula, and has been shown at local galleries and venues. Generally, she says her work has become more abstract with age, but she enjoys working in a variety of styles and media.

Z Morales

Z is a young aspiring artist who works through multimedia

means such as digital painting, illustration and more. With years of practice under their belt, Z now works in a few different art-centered jobs as a teacher for all ages. Z is continuing towards building a bigger portfolio of their work with every school and work project they make.

Tony Moramarco

Tony Moramarco is a native Californian. He has been published as an Artist multiple times and owns and operates Bigfoot Art Classes, in Murrieta, CA. He likes to jump from Cartooning, to Pop Art, to Abstract Art and combine those genres, whenever possible. He has paintings available at **www.GalleryM.com**.

Brooke Olson

Brooke Olson is a 24-year-old artist, local to the Temecula Valley. Inspired by anime and video games, she went on to earn a degree in Entertainment Art/Animation at Cal State Fullerton. She now focuses on personal artistic projects and works at Bigfoot Graphics inspiring young artists to pursue their passion in art.

Kathryn Otoshi

Kathryn Otoshi is an acclaimed children's book author and illustrator, best known for her character-building number book series, *Zero*, *One*, and *Two*. Her upcoming book, *The White Raven*, introduces hope, healing and the power of choice to young readers. She visits schools across the country to foster positive character assets among students and encourage educators to find creative methods to engage their students through art, reading and the power of literature.

Mary Painter

Mary Painter is an international artist who has had art exhibitions in the United States and Japan, where she has both lived and worked for 6 years. A graduate in Studio Art and Environmental Design Studies, she loves all things constructed and loves to paint both analog and digital. When she isn't working on her architectural watercolor series and her original manga, you can find her practicing music, gaming, studying languages, or traveling. Instagram: @primarypainter Website: **marypainter.net**

Kai B. Parker

Kai B. Parker lives in Temecula Valley with 3 dogs and his toy collection. He also has a wife and 2 kids. Kai has been drawing since he could pick up a pencil and enjoys it so much that he gave up his lucrative modeling career to focus on it. Kai describes his art, like his life, as "Simply Complicated." A bunch of little things piled up into a big mess that people can't help but stare at.

Robert Lewis Rieger

Robert Lewis Rieger, born in 1943, writes and publishes children's stories, however he began his creative work from early childhood as an artist, concentrating on oil paintings, pencil drawings and pen and ink.

He considers himself a fine artist rather than an illustrator. Digital art has opened a new world to him, and he has already had one such work published to illustrate a short story he authored for the Temecula Valley Writers and Illustrators.

Charlie Schimmel

Charlie Schimmel is a San Diego-born artist working across both digital and traditional media. His portfolio includes commissioned designs for the Western Science Center and Air Force Navy Task Forces, as well as live caricature art for the City of Temecula and prominent public events. He also serves as an instructor at Bigfoot Art Classes, mentoring students ages 7–60 helping them build confidence across a variety of mediums.

Stefanie Schonleber

Stefanie Schonleber is an artist based in sunny San Diego, CA. Her art is all about capturing the whimsical and colorful moments of life in a realistic way. "Whether it's a landscape, a portrait, or something in between, I aim to infuse my work with a sense of wonder and magic."

Madeline Secules

Madeline Secules is a professional artist, local to the SoCal area. They have previously been published in *Stay Awhile: Vol. 1* anthology, and *Kelly Catches a Leprechaun* by Karen Boyle.

When not drawing lizards, they love fantasy illustration and routinely put their art skills to use drawing DnD chaos, creepy critters, and much more.

They currently work for Bigfoot Graphics, as an art instructor. This will be their second publication with TVWI.

Michael Smith

Michael Smith was a midwestern boy on his own when he got off the Greyhound bus in Pacific Beach, California. The sun, sand, and water immediately felt like home and inspired his art and illustrations. Decades of being a freelance artist led to careers in editorial cartooning and graphic design. His latest endeavor was as a T-shirt designer and screen printer. Acme Screen Printing was his own business for twenty-six years, re-creating other people's designs on T-shirts, at the same time printing his own visions.

His medium is colored pencils/ink which he has plenty of time now to pursue.

John Waddleton

John is an intermittent artist, creating when and if the mood strikes! Having graduated from pencil and pen to an expanded palette upon purchasing his first iPad a few years ago, his recent creations are much more colorful. John's favorite tool is the eraser.

Erin Warren

Erin is a freelance artist who enjoys horror and fantasy work.

Robin Wesley

Robin Wesley has loved arts and crafts her entire life but never thought of herself as artist.

Recently she began a new career as a short storywriter. In the past year she has expanded her creative pursuit to include sketching and watercolors. This is her first published art piece. To see more of her artwork and learn about her journey as a writer visit her website at **www.robinwesleywriter.com**.

Acknowledgments

No book is possible without an incredible amount of sweat, tears, and cussing from a wide range of people and groups.

TVWI would like to thank **Janice Cipriani-Willis** for her time and thoughtful, expert input as the judge and curator throughout the selection process of this anthology. Janice is an award-winning watercolorist who lives and works at Dorland Mountain Arts in Temecula. See her work at **www.janicecipriani.com**.

Jeff Waddleton gave unstintingly of his time and expertise in the planning and layout of LETTERS.

Victor Schmid jumped into the fray, volunteering his expert eyes to help copy edit and proofread.

Thank you to the **City of Temecula** for their unwavering commitment to the arts, culture, and the dreams of TVWI.

And to all the coffee shops of Temecula: we appreciate both the places of gathering with like-minded souls and the caffeine you provide!

Thank you...

...for your purchase of LETTERS.

Art is precious in today's world. Your support of Temecula Valley Writers and Illustrators helps us help creatives.

Please consider leaving a book review on the site from which you purchased this. Reviews are the lifeblood of illustrators; you might be surprised how much extra attention it garners for our contributors.

And, please follow them on their social media handles to see what they are up to next!

Thanks again.
Temecula Valley Writers and Illustrators
"Creativity in Community"

Also Available from TVWI Publishing:

Stay Awhile: Scenes from Temecula Valley

TVWI Book 1: Illustrated Short Stories

Stay Awhile Longer: More Scenes from Temecula Valley

TVWI Book 2: Illustrated Short Stories

Made in United States
Troutdale, OR
08/04/2026

52208474R00069